Islam

The Basics: 2

Islam

Roland Machatschke

SCM PRESS LTD
Trinity Press International

Translated by John Bowden from the German *Islam*, published
1990 in the *kurz und bündig* series by
hpt-Verlagsgesellschaft m.b.H & Co KG, Vienna.

© hpt-Verlagsgesellschaft m.b.H & Co KG, Vienna 1990

Translation © John Bowden 1995

First U.S. edition published 1996
by Trinity Press International, P.O. Box 851, Valley Forge, PA 19482-0851.

Library of Congress Cataloging-in-Publication Data Available.

ISBN 1-56338-162-1 (Trinity Press)

First British edition published 1995 by SCM Press Ltd, 9-17 St. Albans Place,
London N1 0NX

Typeset at The Spartan Press Ltd, Lymington, Hants

96 97 98 99 00 01 02   8 7 6 5 4 3 2 1

Contents

vi   *Contents*

Muhammad and His Teaching

'Praise be to Allah, Lord of the Creation, The Com-
passionate, the Merciful, King of the Last Judgment!
You alone we worship, and to You alone we pray for
help. Guide us to the straight path, the path of those
whom You have favoured, Not of those who have
incurred Your wrath, nor of those who have gone
astray.'

If we replaced 'Allah' by 'God', the origin of this text would
not be immediately obvious. In that case the Al-Fatiha, the
'opening', the first chapter of the holy book of Islam, could
also come from the Bible. This is no coincidence. The man to
whom according to Islamic faith the direct revelations of
God were communicated by the archangel Gabriel, the
prophet Muhammad, stood at the end of a series of
prophets. After Judaism and Christianity, Islam is the
youngest of the three great religions of revelation. Muhammad knew substantial parts of Jewish and Christian
teachings when he experienced his calling and developed a
new teaching. Like Judaism and Christianity, Islam came
into being in the deserts and semi-wildernesses of the
Middle East and, like the Christian religion, it spread all
over the world. Christianity and Islam have something else
in common: in their names streams of blood have flowed!

Muhammad – prophet and founder of a state

Muhammad (= praised be he) was born in Mecca around 570 CE. His father died immediately before or after his son's birth. Both parents were members of the Hashim family, an impoverished subsidiary line of the Quraysh, who ruled Mecca.

In the time of Muhammad Mecca was a trading city at the crossroads of two important caravan routes. One led from north to south from Syria to Palestine and the Yemen, and the other linked East Africa with the Persian Gulf over the Red Sea. The Quraysh, who had developed from camel drivers and caravan escorts into merchants, acted very skilfully. They offered Mecca as a market place and declared four months to be 'holy months' in which there was to be no fighting and even blood vengeance had to pause. This meant that business could develop in peace.

However, above all the Ka'ba made Mecca a focal point. The Ka'ba, an ancient Arabian sanctuary, is a building in the form of a cube, in which originally a multiplicity of gods were worshipped. On the outer wall of the Ka'ba there is a fetish, a black stone, which is probably a meteorite. And in drought-ridden Arabia the never-failing spring of Zamzam in front of the Ka'ba has always contributed to the fame of Mecca as a place of pilgrimage.

Muhammad was around six years old when his mother Amina died. He went first to his grandfather, and after his grandfather's death to his uncle on his father's side, Abu Talib. Abu Talib trained his nephew to be a caravan manager, a dangerous and highly respected profession. Muhammad's life underwent a change when he entered the service of Khadija, the widow of a rich merchant. He finally married her; his wife was fifteen years older than he was.

As a rich merchant Muhammad went into the lands bordering on Arabia and made the acquaintance of foreign cultures and religions. At the beginning of the seventh century there were isolated Christian communities on the Arabian peninsula. However, they were only of any significance in the north, on the frontier with the Byzantine empire, where some Arabian tribes had accepted Christianity. By contrast, there were considerable Jewish communities near Mecca, for example in the city of Yathrib, better known by the name Medina. A third religious group which influenced Muhammad was that of the Hanifs. They proclaimed belief in one God, but were neither Jews nor Christians.

From his youth onwards, Muhammad was evidently in search of God. Time and again he would leave Mecca and withdraw for a few days into the barren hills near the city to meditate. There, at around the age of forty-two, on Mount Hira, he had a key experience. An angel appeared to him in a dream and offered him a scroll containing the words:

'Recite in the name of your Lord, the Creator, who created man from clots of blood. Recite! Your Lord is the Most Bounteous One, who by the pen has taught mankind the things they did not know' (Surah 96, The Blood Clots).

Muhammad woke up, and heard a voice from heaven: 'Muhammad, you are the elect of Allah, and I am Gabriel.'

First of all he told only his wife Khadija about his experience on the mountain. He continued his ascetic practices but was vouchsafed no more appearances and lapsed into depression. However, the angel Gabriel spoke to him a second time:

'By the light of day
and by the fall of night,
your Lord has not forsaken you,
nor does he abhor you.

... You shall be gratified with what your Lord will give you.
Did he not find you an orphan and give you shelter?
Did he not find you in error and guide you?
Did he not find you poor and enrich you?'

(Surah 93, Daylight).

At first Muhammad initiated only a few people into the mystery of the revelations that he had received: in addition to Khadija only those men who after his death were his direct followers as the first caliphs. Only when Muhammad received from God the command 'Arise and give warning' (Surah 74) did he begin to proclaim the revelations publicly. They were above all visions of the end, which the Prophet preached to his followers and opponents in front of the Ka'ba, his gaze turned in the direction of Jerusalem. The last judgment, the final conflagration, the resurrection of the dead, paradise and hell – at that time these were central ingredients of the spiritual world of Christianity and Judaism.

Conflicts soon broke out with the ruling Quraysh, who saw their polytheism – and probably also the lucrative pilgrimages to the Ka'ba – threatened by Muhammad's uncompromising belief in one God – monotheism. Furthermore, Muhammad gained followers above all from the lower social strata. The situation reached such a pitch that Muhammad recommended that his followers should emigrate overseas to Ethiopia. In this difficult period he also suffered two private blows: his wife Khadija and his uncle Abu Talib, who had brought him up, died, one after the other. Again the angel Gabriel intervened. A legend (not the Qur'an) reports that Muhammad was transported by Gabriel to Jerusalem and thence ascended from the sacred rock (which was the site of the temple destroyed by the Romans in 70 CE) to the seventh heaven. There, among others, Adam, Abraham, Moses and Jesus welcomed him as one of them.

Two years later Muhammad's situation in Mecca had become untenable. So he invited his followers to move to the oasis city of Yathrib, which was about 180 miles away. Apart from his family, only a few friends accompanied him in this migration, which resembled a flight. On 20 September 622 his caravan arrived in Yathrib (the city was later renamed 'Medina-en-Nabi', i.e. City of the Prophet). In 638 Caliph Umar fixed the year of the emigration or break (hijra) as the beginning of Muslim chronology.

The years in Medina were decisive not only for the fate of Muhammad's small community but also for the transformation of the new teaching into a world religion. The Prophet proved to be a capable political organizer. He put an end to the controversies in the city and in so doing provided a base for the battle against Mecca. He was not fastidious in choosing his means. The large Jewish community in Medina was partly expelled and partly exterminated. The Jews had provoked Muhammad's wrath because they mocked him for his borrowings from the Old Testament. Nor did they accept his claim to be a prophet in a line with Abraham or Moses. In 624 Muhammad changed the most important elements of the new cult which he had taken over from Judaism. The direction of prayer was shifted from Jerusalem to Mecca; the day of community worship was changed from Saturday to Friday; and the day of fasting was extended to a month of fasting, Ramadan. Islam now put forward the claim to be the only true religion. All the inhabitants of Medina accepted the new faith. The city was now purged of all opponents, governed strictly and given a religious foundation. It could be led into the war against Mecca, the birthplace of the Prophet, which had despised its great son, threatened him and compelled him to flee.

The presupposition for the dissemination of Islam all over the world was a social and political revolution: the abolition of the traditional Arab ties of tribe, kinship and blood, which were replaced by faith. This faith in the one and only God stood so high above all human considerations that there could be only one consequence for those who would not accept it – annihilation. The concept of the 'Holy War' – jihad – developed in Medina for the war against unbelieving Mecca could subsequently be applied to all the campaigns of conquest in the name of Allah.

Muhammad's war against Mecca at first had varying fortunes. Caravans were ambushed and there were minor skirmishes. The troops of both city states besieged each other. In 629 Muhammad negotiated a ten-year cease-fire with his ancestral city, in order to be able to make a pilgrimage with his followers to the Ka'ba. A year later Mecca was his. The city opened its gates to him and his troops after he had promised to spare those inhabitants who accepted Islam.

Muhammad went to the Ka'ba and destroyed the pagan idols in person. Only the 'black stone' was left. In the revelation the Ka'ba – as emerges from the second surah – is 'Abraham's place', which had been desecrated by the idolaters. This view is closely connected with the faith of the Muslims that once there was a kind of monotheistic 'primal religion' from which Jews and Christians also drew parts of their revelations. But God had called Muhammad to free the falsified teaching from all deviations and restore it to its original, pure form.

In the last two years of his life Muhammad devoted himself to the dissemination of Islam on the Arabian peninsula. The Bedouin tribes accepted the new faith, and gradually the beginnings of an Islamic constitution developed which had only loose political links with Muhammad's capital of Medina. However, it had a uniform religious basis The inhabitants of conquered territories could also submit without accepting Islam. In his domain, Muhammad introduced a poll tax for Christians and Jews in the form of money and natural produce. Conquered land belonged to him. He also had a certain proportion of all offerings. Thus many administrative structures of the later Islamic states go back to him.

In 632 Muhammad led an enormous procession of 90,000 pilgrims to Mecca. Shortly after his return to Medina he fell sick, and on 8 June 632 died in the arms of his favourite wife Aisha. He was buried where he died, in his home. As Muhammad's abode was incorporated into the complex of the great mosque of Medina, his tomb today is also in the precincts of the mosque. It is surrounded by a lattice on which is repeated the statement of faith: 'There is no god but Allah, and Muhammad is his Prophet.'

The Qur'an – the holy scripture of the Muslims

The revelations granted to Muhammad are collected in the Qur'an. They are written down in the Prophet's own words. However, for Muslims the Qur'an is not a human work but literally the Word of God.

The English translation of the word Qur'an is 'recitation' or 'reading'. Originally 'Qur'an' may have denoted the individual revelations, but later the meaning was extended. Now 'Qur'an' refers to the whole revelation as book (kitab). When Muhammad died in 632 there was no authoritative collection of his words. They had primarily been preserved in the memory of reciters. Some had also been put down in writing. We know of five such collections of individual Qur'an pages. Soon uncertainties arose as to the correctness of the rendering of the words of the Prophet. Caliph Uthman, Muhammad's third successor, therefore had an official edition of the Qur'an prepared. The collection made by Hafsa, one of the Prophet's wives, was chosen as the basis of the text. A commission worked on collecting and editing for five years. Its Qur'an is the version which is now accepted today. The cities of Mecca, Medina, Damascus, Basra and Kufar, the most important cities of the Islamic empire at the time, each received a copy of the book.

Thus only two decades after the death of Muhammad a binding account of the revelations transmitted to him had been created. However, the text was by no means clear. The reason for this is the peculiarity of Arab script, which above all to begin with had signs only for consonants. It was only very much later that the vowels, too, were preserved in writing. So the text of the Qur'an was 'created' anew each time when it was presented by the reciter. As a result there are many readings which left, and still leave, room for interpretation and speculation. In order to limit excesses in the exegesis of the Qur'an an attempt was made to standardize the readings. From the tenth century on there have been seven schools, which are still taught today. According to Islamic tradition the written version is only a support for the memory. It is learned by reciting for recitation, and presented in a distinctive solemn style.

Until a few years ago the earliest examples of the text of the Qur'an were to be found in Istanbul, to which the fragments had been brought at the end of the nineteenth century after a fire in the Great Mosque of Damascus. Scholarly work has been done on these texts for thirty years. However, at least as important is a wealth of fragments which were recently found in the Great Mosque of Sana in Northern Yemen.

The Qur'an is written in rhymed prose. Since the first complete transmission of the text under Caliph Uthman it has been divided into 114 sections – surahs. With the exception of the first surah ('The opening'), the surahs are arranged by a purely external criterion, according to their extent. The longest are at the beginning, the shortest at the end. 113 of the 114 surahs begin with the words 'In the name of Allah, the merciful'.

Since according to Islamic theology the Qur'an is the word of God revealed through the prophet Muhammad, there are special regulations for it. The Qur'an may not be kept with other books. Words at the end of a line may not be divided. Muslims may not use a translation. That has led to the fact that Muslims with no command of Arabic have to learn the text by heart mechanically, without understanding it.

The Qur'an was translated into Latin as early as the twelfth century. This translation was printed by a Basel printer in 1543 on the basis of a recommendation by Martin Luther. The first Qur'an in German appeared in Nuremberg in 1616. It was based on an Italian text which in turn was based on the old Latin text. The first German Qur'an was published in Frankfurt in 1772, and had been translated from the original Arabic.

The interpretation of the Qur'an is a science in itself. A thirty-volume work has come down to us from as long ago as the tenth century. Countless commentaries have appeared over the centuries. However, there has been historical-critical study of the Qur'an only since the last century. Of course interpretations also pursue superficially political aims, above all when it is a question of giving an Islamic trend or sect legitimacy by the word of the Prophet. The Shi'ites with their different variants in particular emphasized and still emphasize this.

Alongside the Qur'an, the immediate word of God, there are also so-called stories – Hadith. These are reports and legends about Muhammad which were originally handed down by word of mouth and only later put in writing. They refer to contemporaries of Muhammad, primarily his immediate successors as leaders of the Islamic community, the first four caliphs. They had become members of the Prophet's family by marriage. Through the Hadith above all, the person of Muhammad comes to life for believing Muslims.

The principles of Islam

When Muhammad felt called to be a prophet, Arabia had no religious unity. An original polytheism had been partly destroyed, replaced by the two monotheistic religions, Judaism and Christianity. Whole tribes of Bedouins had gone over to Christianity. Christian Arab princely houses ruled in northern Arabia. There were large Jewish communities in oases and cities. The Hanifs, already mentioned, who lived above all in Syria, adopted a position midway between Judaism and Christianity. They believed in one God, Allah.

Allah had already been a deity in Arabia before the appearance of Muhammad. Moreover the Ka'ba was dedicated to him in Mecca. Muhammad made Allah the sole God, not completely abolishing the character of the old world of polytheism but subordinating it to Allah: the spirits, the devil and the angels, who are still elements of the religious cosmos of Islam.

The conflict which flared up over Salman Rushdie's book *The Satanic Verses* has brought to light a little-known chapter in the history of the Qur'an. The 'Satanic verses' are texts which were not included in the current version of the Qur'an. In the view of experts, they represent Muhammad's attempt to come to terms with some of the important representatives of the old world of the gods on the way to uncompromising monotheism. These verses were an abomination to his strict successors, to whom the Christian God split into three persons already smacked of idolatry. So they interpreted them as a 'false revelation', an attempt of

Satan to corrupt the transmission of God's word to
Muhammad, and deleted them. That is one of the reasons –
though not the only one – for the fanatical repudiation of
Rushdie's book in the Islamic world.

Muhammad did not see himself as the creator but as the
perfecter of a religion which had also been revealed to
Abraham, Moses, Elijah and other Jewish prophets, and
finally to Jesus. Muhammad imagined as the source of the
Islamic doctrine of salvation a book in heaven, the 'mother
of books' (umm al-kitab): a primal version of the holy
scriptures of the Jews and Christians. However, these
religions had falsified the word, so Muhammad was called
to proclaim the pure doctrine. For Muslims this pure
doctrine is exclusively contained in the Qur'an, the direct
word of God. Still, as those to whom parts of the one true
faith have come, Jews and Christians are tolerated in Islamic
society as 'people of the book'.

The view of the only God stands at the centre of Islamic
faith. It is formulated most clearly in Surah 112, which is
therefore also called the 'Islamic creed'.

> Say, 'God is One, the Eternal God. He begot none, nor
> was He begotten. None is equal to him.'

This is not only a repudiation of any form of polytheism but
also a clear repudiation of the Christian doctrine of God the
Father, God the Son and God the Holy Spirit.

'Allah' occurs in the Qur'an 2,685 times. The word rarely
stands alone. Allah's ninety-nine names (e.g. the Merciful,
the Lord of the Worlds, the Almighty, the Exalted) set side
by side produce the pearls of the Islamic 'rosary'. God has
created everything: heaven, earth, plants, animals and
human beings. He has given human beings the capacity to
distinguish good from evil. Both tendencies, towards good
and towards evil, are present in human beings from birth

on. It is the duty of human beings to develop the good inclinations in themselves and so live in accord with the divine order.

Fate is particularly important in Islamic doctrine. Human fate is governed both by one's own striving and also by factors over which men and women have no influence. Time and again Islamic theologians have discussed the question whether God has predestined all that happens or whether human beings can take their fate into their own hands. The Qur'an does not give a clear answer. There is evidence for both views. According to the present-day view, human beings are obliged to do their best. The real boundary between being able and not being able is known only to God. God has also given each person special gifts which influence the course of his life. The doctrine of kismet (literally 'portion') in its usual meaning is not rooted in the Qur'an but might be a lapse into pre-Islamic ideas of fatalism. Surrender to an unfathomable destiny, the belief that in any case everything is predestined by Allah, this passivity of thought and action, are features of Islamic life which emerged only in the period of decline and came to be emphasized particularly strongly in the nineteenth century, when the European powers turned almost the whole of the Islamic world into colonies.

Like Christianity, Islam teaches that human existence does not end with death. The other world and the existence of human beings in the other world before the last judgment have an important place in the revelations. Good and evil words will be weighed at the judgment. During their lives sinners can turn to God at any time and at any place, repent of their sins and ask for forgiveness. This forgiveness is always given. In the Sunni tendency of Islam there is even a view that it is enough to confess the principles of Islam to get to Paradise. Granted, great sinners must spend a certain period in hell, but they will be redeemed if Muhammad prays for them as intercessor to God.

Hell is the place where only unbelievers must spend their eternal life. By contrast, believing Muslims cross the torments of hell on a bridge which is narrower than a hair and sharper than the blade of a sword. Paradise is a place of earthly joys. There milk and honey, water and wine flow, and the beautiful women of Paradise (houris) sweeten eternal life for Muslim men:

> Eat and drink to your hearts' content. This is the reward of your labours.
> They shall recline on couches ranged in rows.
> To dark-eyed houris We shall wed them (Surah 52).

Up to the day of the resurrection, dead Muslims rest unconscious in the tomb. Only those who have fallen in the jihad, in the Holy War, go straight to paradise. With this attraction before their eyes, millions and millions of men have gone to their deaths, and not just in the centuries of Islamic expansion. Thus in our day the Khomeini regime in Iran sent its child soldiers into battle against highly-armed Iraq and gave them, as a mockery, little plastic keys with 'the key to paradise' on them.

For Muslims, the Qur'an is not only the source of faith but also the source of law according to which the life of each individual and the communal life of men and women in Islamic society and also religious duties are regulated. These religious duties are summed up in the 'five pillars' on which Islam rests:

1. The shahada – the confession of faith

It consists of the statement: 'I bear witness that there is no God but God and that Muhammad is the Messenger of God.'

2. Salat – prayer

The three daily prayers prescribed in the early period were extended to five. Their outward form is an alternation of standing, bowing and prostration. Before prayer ritual purification is prescribed; in default of water, this may be performed with sand. Since Muhammad's conflict with the Jews in Medina, the direction prescribed for prayer has been the Ka'ba in Mecca. Friday is the main day of prayer. The Muslim can say his prayers anywhere. The mosque is a special place of prayer. The first surah of the Qur'an must be recited at each prayer and also the confession of faith mentioned above. Hours of prayer are before dawn, at midday, three hours after midday, at sunset, and two hours after sunset. At least forty men must be present at Friday prayer in the mosque. Worship is led by an imam, who usually also preaches from the pulpit. The imam is not a priest. he is usually the most learned and most respected member of the congregation.

3. Zakat – alms

Alms were originally voluntary offerings which over the course of time developed into a compulsory offering. This tax for the poor is now collected by the Islamic state and is part of taxation generally. It amounts to 2.5% annually of the value of the property, other possessions and income of a Muslim who has been free of debt for a year. Agricultural products are taxed at 10% if irrigation is natural and 5% if it is artificial.

4. Sawm – fasting

Instead of the original fast day on the Jewish model, Muhammad proscribed a month of fasting – Ramadan.

This is the ninth month of the Islamic lunar year which because of the peculiarities of the lunar calendar can fall in any season. The Qur'an is said to have been sent to earth during a month of fasting. Fasting also includes refraining from smoking and sexual intercourse. It applies during the day between dawn and sunset.

5. Hajj – the pilgrimage

This is prescribed once in the life of every adult Muslim. Poverty and sickness bring exemption from this duty. This pilgrimage to Mecca in the last month of the lunar year strengthens the sense of solidarity among Muslims from the most varied cultures. Two days' march from Mecca the pilgrim puts on a garment made of two seamless pieces of white cloth. When he enters the precinct of the mosque in Mecca he washes himself and his head-dress with water from the spring Zamzam. Then he circles the Ka'ba in the middle of the broad courtyard seven times anti-clockwise and kisses the 'black stone' in the wall of the Ka'ba. After that he walks fast seven times between the two hillocks Safa and Marwa. On the eighth day he prays from noon to sunset on the hill of Arafat. Then he visits Mina in the desert and puts stones on three heaps (a symbolic stoning of the devil). On the tenth day of the pilgrimage month the sacrificial feast is celebrated. The pilgrims to Mecca and those who have remained at home slaughter an animal and give the flesh to the poor.

These 'five pillars of faith' also include the duty of the holy war – jihad. This is war against the unbelievers, the non-Muslims, required in some surahs. The obligation to take part in the jihad was one of the most important factors in the explosive spread of Islam, above all at the beginning. Today

Islamic theologians interpret the jihad as the battle against injustice, need, hunger, and for defence and liberation.

For Shi'ites there is a further duty: belief in the imams.

But the Qur'an is not just a codex of religious and moral duties. Since in Islam community and state are identical, the social life of Muslims is also regulated by the laws of Allah as proclaimed to his prophet Muhammad. The term 'Shari'a' has been coined for the totality of these precepts.

The Shari'a is criminal, family, inheritance, civil and property law. It regulates behaviour towards non-Muslims, and it contains dietary laws (e.g. a prohibition against eating pork and drinking wine) and regulations for slaughtering animals. Nowhere in the Islamic world are the requirements of the Shari'a fulfilled literally. It is clear even to Islamic states with a 'fundamentalist' orientation that a lawbook which was essentially completed in the ninth century cannot be applied without changes to the social conditions of the twentieth century. Many theologians also see the draconian punishments of the Shari'a (cutting off hands and feet, stoning and the like) as outdated. It is probably no coincidence that states which appealed or appeal especially to the Shari'a are or were socially more repressive (Iran, Sudan, Pakistan, Libya, Saudi Arabia, to mention just a few).

Gambling is also forbidden in Islam, which is why orthodox Muslims reject insurance schemes – and usury – so that until recently there was no banking system in the Islamic world. These are examples of the way in which religious precepts prove a restraining influence on development in a world in which of course a good deal has changed over the more than 1,350 years since Muhammad.

In connection with the re-Islamicization which has taken place since the 1970s, increased attention has been paid to Islamic law. One great problem is that the Qur'an gives an answer to only a tiny proportion of legal questions. Thus in many states, above all in those which had a long association with a European colonial power, principles of Islamic law exist alongside laws which have been shaped by the European philosophy of law. On the other hand, these states in particular are striving to overcome their identity crisis by an intensive return to the roots, i.e. to Islam.

In family law, which has the closest tie to religion, the main problem is that the laws of marriage have to be adapted to the changed social conditions. Throughout the Islamic world – including the two 'socialist' states of Somalia and the People's Republic of Yemen – the husband is the head of the family. The wife is obliged to obey and follow him. In most Islamic states the husband may repudiate his wife. Often, however, a legal hearing must take place. Usually an attempt at reconciliation must follow; a passage in the Qur'an is support for this. In Egypt a husband can repudiate his wife without giving any reason, as in the old days, but he must have his action officially registered and inform his wife of it if she was not personally present when he repudiated her. High compensation for wives who are repudiated without cause is meant to make divorce difficult.

Polygamy is also officially being made difficult all over the Islamic world, though only in Tunisia has it been explicitly abolished by the legislation. In many countries, however, a second marriage must be legally approved. In Egypt the husband who wants to take a second wife must give evidence of an already successful marriage, so that the first wife can be officially advised. In some states the first wife has the right to apply for divorce if her husband takes a second wife. According to Islamic law it is even possible to enter into a third and fourth marriage. However, this is not provided for in the family law of present-day Islamic states. Evidently the basic presupposition is that on economic grounds nowadays it is possible for very few people to treat several wives equally, as the Qur'an prescribes. Only the Prophet himself had more than four wives. God himself reflected on Muhammad's harem and in addition to his share of the plunder from military campaigns allowed him 'any believing woman who gives herself to the prophet and whom the Prophet wishes to take in marriage. This privilege is yours alone, being granted to no other believer' (Surah 33). When Muhammad died, he was mourned by nine widows.

Political events in some Islamic states have focussed interest very strongly on Islamic penal law. Most Islamic states have had a penal law with clearly European features since the 1950s and 1960s. It also often continues to exist in countries which have officially reintroduced Islamic law. Only in Saudi Arabia and Oman does exclusively Islamic law apply.

In the Qur'an itself five punishable offences are listed:

1. Illicit sexual relations: death by stoning is the penalty for adultery, in other cases flogging.
2. Slander involving alleged illicit sexual relations: flogging.
3. Drinking wine (the prohibition applies to all alcoholic drinks): flogging.
4. Theft: penalties differ widely depending on the nature of the crime, the value of the stolen object and the link between perpetrator and victim; when applied rigorously the penalty is the amputation of the right hand for the first offence and the left foot for a subsequent offence.
5. Street robbery: depending on the type of crime (ranging from simple mugging to killing), imprisonment, amputation of hands and feet, execution and crucifixion.

The old Arab principle of blood vengeance for killing another person has been heavily qualified in Islam. It is still the case that the nearest male relative of the victim may carry out the death penalty by the sword with his own hands once judgment has been pronounced, under the supervision of the judge. Similarly, in the case of bodily injury there is a right to inflict on the perpetrator the same injuries as were inflicted on the victim. This kind of retribution can also be replaced by compensation through the 'blood price'. Traffic accidents with fatal consequences do not fall under the law of blood vengeance. Apostasy from Islam is punishable by death – the best known case in recent times is the death penalty pronounced against the writer Salman Rushdie by Ayatollah Khomeini.

The strict penalties in Islam contrast with a judicial procedure which is very much in favour of the accused. As a rule a verdict can be given only on the basis of a confession, and confessions can be retracted. However, we know through the work of Amnesty International the way in which confessions are often gained. In punishing the five 'Qur'anic' offences there is a tendency towards leniency; in other words, death penalties are commuted. The discretion of the judge, which in any case is absolute in judgments on other crimes, can increasingly also be applied in the case of these crimes.

To Western European legal sensibilities Islamic criminal law contains many contradictions and features of particular cruelty. The harsh penalties are meant to serve as deterrents. Changes are provided for only in a qualified way. Just as religion and state are inseparable in Islam, so too law and religion hang together. Konrad Dilger, a German expert on Islamic law, argues that: 'Dispensing with the cruel penalties of Islamic penal law would represent an elimination of the irrational elements of Islam and the dissolution of its religious character. The death penalty in particular seems to be an inseparable ingredient of Islam.'

Islam regulates the whole life of its followers, both personal and corporate. A separation of state and church of the kind that occurs in the Western Christian world is unthinkable for a Muslim. For the laws under which he lives are the work of God. Unconditional belief in the Qur'an as the Word of God was one of the reasons for the rapid militant spread of Islam. The social elements of its teaching have maintained their attraction, above all for people in the Third World. Problems which arise from applying the authentic word which has been laid down for more than 1,300 years to new social developments have often remained unresolved.

2

Tendencies and Schools

Only a generation after the death of Muhammad, Islam was no longer a united faith. A dispute flared up over the question of who was to succeed the Prophet. Today the two main tendencies in Islam – Sunna and Shi'a – while agreed on the principles of the teaching of the Qur'an, differ in its interpretation, especially in connection with leadership of the community. Around 83% of all Muslims are Sunnis, and about 15% Shi'ites. The remaining 2% belong to sects.

Sunni Islam – the traditional tendency

The Arabic word sunna means custom or tradition. So by European concepts Sunnis are orthodox.

Within Sunni Islam there are four schools of law. The most important of them is the Hanafite school of law, named after Imam Abu Hanifa, who taught in the eighth century. It is followed by more than 42% of Muslims and is thus numerically the strongest group in Islam. It recognizes personal opinion and the social compatibility of a solution alongside Qur'an and Sunna as a means of establishing the law.

As in Christianity, so too in Islam a mystical ascetic trend developed at a very early stage. Since the tenth century it has been called Sufism. Its most important representative is Husain ibn Mansur al-Hallaj, who was executed as a heretic in 922. He was a man with great charisma and a sense of social mission.

Finally in the thirteenth century the Islamic brotherhoods came into being. They were like religious orders and members of them were later called dervishes in Europe. The orders can be distinguished by their cultic practices and their clothing. The 'dancing dervishes' fall into ecstasy by dancing, while the 'howling dervishes' cultivate a special kind of music and song in their religious practices.

Shi'ite Islam – a name for many tendencies

In the year 656 the third successor of the Prophet, Caliph Uthman, was murdered. His successor, Ali ibn Abi Talib, was recognized only by part of the community. The governor of Syria, Mu'awiya, from the house of the Umayyads, rebelled against him. Ali was assassinated, and his sons Hasan and Husayn – their mother was Muhammad's daughter Fatima – fell in battle with the Umayyads.

The Shi'ites are convinced that Muhammad's son-in-law Ali should have been the Prophet's first successor. They support their conviction with quotations from the Qur'an and with statements from the tradition (Hadith). The designation Shi'a derives from shi'at Ali (Ali's party). In contrast to the Sunnis, who recognize the first four successors of Muhammad, including Ali, as the 'rightly guided caliphs', the Shi'ites reject Ali's three predecessors as usurpers.

The most important religious and political characteristic of Shi'ite Islam must be seen as the unqualified authority of the imam, the spiritual leader of a community. Only someone who can trace his descent directly from the Prophet through Ali and his wife Fatima can be imam.

The Shi'a is spilt into several tendencies, the most important of which is the 'twelver' Shi'a. The Iranians, for example, are twelver Shi'ites. The supporters of this tendency of the Shi'a believe in a series of twelve imams, beginning with Ali. The most important figure in this series is Ali's son (Muhammad's grandson) Husayn, who was defeated along with his small army by his Umayyad enemies at Kerbala (in present-day Iraq) in 680. The day of Husayn's death is celebrated by the Shi'ites every year as the 'day of the martyrs' with processions, flagellations and passion plays, in which the waves of religious ecstasy rise particularly high. The eleventh imam in this series died in 874 and according to the teaching of the twelver Shi'a his successor, the twelfth imam, has been kept alive by God in a miraculous way and still is alive today as the hidden imam. This twelfth imam is the Mahdi, the ruler of the whole earth at the end of the world. In his absence the community is led by the mullahs. Above all in Iran all clergy are called mullahs. Anyone who achieves a higher theological status – though there are no fixed criteria for this – is given the title Ayatollah. Khomeini was also often called imam, but this only meant that he was regarded as the supreme religious and secular authority, as it were as 'representative' of the hidden twelfth imam.

In addition to the martyr cult, which is of great importance above all for the mass of simple people, the twelver Shi'a is characterized by a marked veneration of tombs. A sharp contrast with the Sunnis, to whom such a cult is alien, has developed here. Therefore the antipathy of the Iranian Shi'ites to the Sunni Saudis as guardians of the holy places goes far deeper than everyday politics. The Shi'ites cannot forgive the Wahhabis (supporters of the dominant Sunni tendency in Saudi Arabia) for having allowed the cupolas over the tombs in Medina to be destroyed in 1926.

The tendencies within the Shi'a are named after the number of the imams that they recognize: the fiver Shi'a (Zaydis) and the sevener Shi'a (Ismailis). Further splits developed directly or indirectly from the latter. These include the Fatimids, who ruled in Egypt from the tenth to

the twelfth century and dominated the bordering areas of
North Africa, the Druze (mainly to be found in Lebanon),
and the faith community of the Aga Khan with its centre in
Pakistan.

Sects – the results of schisms

A number of branches which are still significant have
developed from one of the oldest tendencies in Islam, the
Kharijites. In addition to the Ibadis, who have their
stronghold in Oman, mention should be made here of the
Wahhabis. Their tendency has been the state religion in
Saudi Arabia since the establishment of the kingdom. Their
founder, the Qur'anic scholar Muhammad ibn Abd al-
Wahhab, represented a strict monotheism which condemned the worship of saints as heresy. In the middle of the
eighteenth century Wahhab won over the ruling Saud
family to his teaching. A certain militant tendency drove the
Wahhabis to subject Muslims who had other beliefs. They
were understood as 'unbelievers', against whom it was a
religious duty to wage war.

The sect of the Yazidis has been abandoned to an evil fate.
They are rejected and persecuted by both the Muslims and
the Christians of their environment. A contributory factor
here is that the Yazidis belong above all to the people of the
Kurds, a people which for centuries has been the plaything
of greater peoples and has hardly any prospect of every
establishing its own state. The Yazidis have moved far from
original Islam, but it nevertheless forms the basis of their
faith, though mixed with Christian and ancient Persian
(Zoroastrian) elements. They do not worship the devil or
the stars at all – as their enemies claim. Their religion
imposes very high moral and ethical demands on them.
Certain peculiarities, which are to be explained from
outside pressure, make the Yazidis even more suspect to

their neighbours. Thus they keep their religion secret and marry only within their community. In Turkey, where most Yazidis live, they are cruelly persecuted – despite the fact that since Ataturk's revolution the Turkish Republic has been officially non-religions. Hostility is taken so far that doctors in Turkish hospitals even refuse to treat Yazidis.

The Baha'is, an idealistic religious community with pacifist inclinations, who are so tolerant that their temples are open to all, developed from the Shi'a. The sect of the Baha'is came into being around the middle of the nineteenth century in Iran. Its origin is closely connected with the belief of the Shi'ites in the ruler of the end-time, the Mahdi. The basis of Baha'ism is the 'Bab' (Gate), a secret confidant of the twelfth, hidden imam, who is to bring about access to the Mahdi himself. The Baha'is know no resurrection, no paradise and no hell, but believe that through the grace of God human beings grow to perfection after death. The Baha'is practise mission, are deeply committed to social and charitable work and attach great importance to education. In their homeland Iran they have always been persecuted, and it is not surprising that under Khomeini's regime this persecution was resumed with new fanaticism.

The sect of the Ahmadis similarly emerged in the nineteenth century. Their founder was an Indian who saw himself not only as Mahdi but also as Jesus redivivus and the incarnation of Krishna. The Ahmadis reject the jihad and want to spread Islam peacefully. They have about five million adherents in Pakistan and are split into two tendencies.

Sunna and Shi'a are the best-known tendencies in Islam today. Disputes over the faith broke out immediately after the death of Muhammad. In an unofficial tradition he himself prophesied the division of Islam into seventy-one sects. The individual trends in Islam are marked by great intolerance towards one another.

3

Dissemination

The rapid spread of Islam in the seventh century and the rise of a great Arab empire under the banner of the Prophet are tremendous historical events which have had an effect down to our own day. Within the space of only three generations members of the nomadic tribes conquered an empire which embraced the Middle East and the southern Mediterranean. The Arab empire from the frontiers of India to the Atlantic was won in battle against the two most powerful states of the world of the time: Byzantium and Persia.

Arabia and the Middle East – the cradle of Islam

After the revival of Persia in the third century CE the age-old cultural area between the eastern Mediterranean and the land enclosed by the rivers Euphrates and Tigris became the arena in which the power interests of the Roman empire and the empire of the Persian Sassanids clashed. The conflicts lasted for centuries and outlived the end of the Roman empire. Byzantium entered into the heritage of the Roman empire and continued the war, which was never clearly decided. At the beginning of the seventh century the Persians besieged Byzantium which then, from the year 622 – under Emperor Herakleios – gained a breathing space with a counter-offensive. Muhammad also took part in this war for domination in his own capacity as leader of his community. Muhammad was on the Byzantine side. Historians conjecture that the reason for this was his disagreement with the Jews in Medina. The Jews supported Persia and were cruelly persecuted throughout the Byzantine empire after the Byzantine victory in 630.

After the capitulation of Mecca in 630 and the consolidation of his secular power, Muhammad planned to extend the 'orthodox' faith, if need be with the sword. The interests of Byzantium were not affected while the action remained on the Arabian peninsula – Arabia was too far away. However, when the hosts of the prophets turned northwards, they inevitably came into conflict with Byzantium.

Muhammad died before the campaign could begin. His successor, Abu Bakr, the first caliph, reigned for only two years. However, this period was enough to introduce the great revolutions at the end of which the Mediterranean area was to look quite different. In 634 Arab troops were in Mesopotamia, in Syria and in Palestine. Only Jerusalem still offered resistance.

Two factors favoured the Arabs: Byzantium and Persia were weakened by the war between them, and Arab mercenaries who had fought on both sides had returned home with an excellent knowledge of modern warfare. But above all there was the impetus of faith. Allah required that his followers should convert unbelievers, if need be with the sword. And he promised a reward in the world to come for those who took part in the Holy War. In the words of the Qur'an:

'When you meet the unbelievers in the battlefield strike off their heads, until you have laid them low . . .

As for those who are slain in the cause of Allah, He will not allow their works to perish. He will vouchsafe them guidance and ennoble their state; He will admit them to Paradise . . .' (Surah 47).

Umar, the second Caliph, continued the work of Abu Bakr.

Two victories in battle opened up wider historical prospects. A Byzantine army was defeated at the river Yarmuk, between the Jordan and Lake Gennesaret. The whole of Syria and Palestine fell into the hands of the Arabs. The way to Egypt was clear. In present-day Iraq an Arab army defeated a Persian force with superior arms. The Sassanid king Yazdegerd III was murdered by his own people. Persia lay open to the Arabs.

The conquest of Persia was the work of the third caliph, Uthman, who was elected successor to the murdered Umar in 644. (He is already known to us for his achievement in the history of religion, namely fixing the Qur'an in writing.) Under Uthman the attempt was first made to invade southwards up the Nile from Egypt. But the Arabs failed to overcome the resistance of the Christian empire of Nubia on the upper Nile.

The Arab army operated with greater success on its campaign from Egypt westwards. After bloody battles with the Berbers it finally reached the Atlantic.

The empire of the Umayyads – from the Atlantic to eastern Persia

Uthman's successor, who was murdered in 656. was Muhammad's cousin and son-in-law Ali. However, his election was contested by Mu'awiya, the governor in Syria, who came from the family of the Umayyads. A civil war over the Prophet's successor stopped the Arabic expansion for a time. The most important consequence of this confusion within Arabia was the division of Islam into the two main tendencies of Sunni and Shi'a.

Ali died in 661, as we heard, at the hand of assassins; Mu'awiya became caliph and founded the dynasty of the Umayyads.

Under the Umayyads the Islamic conquests developed

into an Arab empire. Arabic was declared the state language. The conversion of unbelievers to Islam was no longer the urgent aim of the military campaigns. Only Arabs could be Muslims and bear weapons. As warriors they had to be provided for by their subjects. A uniform coinage was introduced to reinforce the idea of a central empire. The rule of the Umayyads was characterized by tolerance to those of other beliefs, i.e. Christians and Jews. These paid a poll tax and land tax and enjoyed the protection of the Islamic state, which – in contrast to the Byzantine empire – did not force its faith on them. That also applied to the Christians in Palestine and Egypt, who had suffered under the attempts of Byzantium to convert them to the Greek rite.

At the beginning of the eighth century the internal Arab disputes had been sufficiently settled for it to be possible to think again of extending Islam with fire and sword. In 711 the general Tariq Ibn Ziyad crossed from North Africa into Spain. Since then the strait between Africa and Europe has borne his name – Gibraltar (which derives from the Arab name for the dominant rock on the Spanish side, Jabal Tariq). Roderick, king of the West Goths, was defeated in battle at the river Salado, and was killed in the fighting.

The Arabs rapidly conquered the Iberian peninsula. Only in the extreme north-west was a small Christian state able to survive. In a skirmish which has been handed down in a partly legendary tradition, Count Pelagius (Spanish Pelayo) of the West Goths defeated an Arab army. Christian history saw this as a turning point in the reconquest of Spain by the Christians, the Reconquistà. It was to take 781 years, for only in 1492 did the Arab (Moorish) rule in Spain end with the capitulation of Granada.

The Arabs did not stop even at the Pyrenees and invaded southern France. From the Mediterranean they reached Narbonne and Toulouse, but were unable to keep a footing there for long. Further west they penetrated deeper into

France, since the kingdom of the Franks had been weakened for decades by internal conflicts. At the beginning of the eighth century the Carolingians had emerged victors from the bitter struggle for control, which was nominally exercised by insignificant representatives of the royal house of the Merovingians. When after a lengthy pause an Arab army set out under a new and fanatical leader, the Frankish kingdom was armed and ready to defend itself. A strong personality guided the fortunes of the emperor as steward (major domo): Charles Martel (= Hammer). He assembled an army and with the insights of a brilliant strategist chose the right place to face the enemy. This was a marshy area at the confluence of two streams near the city of Tours. It gave the rapid Arab cavalry no possibility of exploiting its superiority. The two armies camped opposite each other for seven days. Then on 17 October 732 came the battle. The Arabs suffered a devastating defeat and slowly retreated over the Pyrenees to Spain.

The battle of Tours was one of those events which decide the course of history: the Arabs accepted the Pyrenees as the frontier of their sphere of power. The Christian resistance fighters, who were concentrated in the inaccessible north-west corner of Spain, drew courage, and the Frankish kingdom was able to continue the process of consolidation towards becoming a major European power. Charlemagne, Charles Martel's grandson, established the Spanish Mark, one of the centres of the Reconquistà, between the Pyrenees and the Ebro.

It would be quite wrong to see Arab rule in Spain as a period of oppression, as a one-sided account of Christian history has done. The splendid era of the Umayyads was also a heyday for Spain.

Around the middle of the eighth century rebellions and unrest in various parts of the giant Umayyad empire heralded the coming end of an era. In 750 the last Umayyad caliph, Marwan II, was defeated and murdered as he fled. A new dynasty of rulers entered the history of the Islamic world, the Abbasids, who derived their name from Abbas, an uncle of the Prophet. The Umayyad family was systematically exterminated. Only a single Umayyad, Abd-al-Rahman, succeeded in fleeing to Spain, where in 756 he founded a kingdom in Cordoba.

Arab rule in Spain was marked by special tolerance: Christians were not only allowed to practise their religion without hindrance but could also retain their legal system. Trade and craftsmanship flourished. Cordoba was a centre of the silk and leather industry. Almeria was famed for its ceramics and Toledo for its weapons industry. Especially in Andalucia agriculture profited from the highly-developed Arab methods of irrigation. Arab scholars brought their superior knowledge of medicine, astronomy and mathematics to Europe. Arab philosophers cultivated the works of Plato and Aristotle, with whom the West which had become Christian no longer wanted anything to do.

The Umayyads operated less successfully in the East than in the West. Certainly all the possessions of Byzantium, the great enemy, had been seized in the Near East; Crete and Cyprus had been conquered; and the empire which not long before had been so powerful was reduced to the city of Constantinople. However, the warriors under the banner of the Prophet came to grief over the greatest city of the world at that time. An Arab fleet besieged Constantinople from 673 to 677. The Byzantines defended themselves successfully with the help of the invention of a Syrian architect, 'Greek fire', a highly inflammable chemical combination which even continued to burn on water. This was an unbeatable 'secret weapon' against wooden ships. In 717 the Arabs stood for a second time before the walls of Constantinople. There a new, wise and vigorous emperor had ascended the throne: Leo III, called the Isaurian. He broke the siege. This event was as important for the East of Europe as the victory of Charles Martel at Tours had been for the West. The Arabs did not appear before Constantinople a third time.

In Asia enormous areas were won for Islam. From Persia, Islamic armies penetrated to Central Asia and conquered Transoceania with its famous cities of Samarkand and Bukhara. In Central Asia the Muslims came in contact with various Turkish peoples. The conversion of these peoples became the basis of one of the strongest impulses for the military dissemination of Islam.

At the time when Tariq was crossing the Straits of Gibraltar in the West, the Emirate of Muitan was founded in the remote valley of the Indus far in the East – the basis of the later Islamic India of the Moguls.

The empire of the Abbasids

Abu al-Abbas, the founder of the Abbasid dynasty, transferred the capital of the Islamic empire from Damascus to Baghdad, a newly-created residence on the Tigris. In the ninth century there was a new wave of Islamic expansion in southern Europe which began from North Africa. The Arabs had developed into a sea power in the Mediterranean, and their fleets conquered the Balearic Islands, Corsica, Sardinia, Sicily and Malta. Today a language influenced by Arabic is still spoken on Malta. An emirate could even establish itself on the Italian peninsula for three decades (Bari, 841–871).

In the tenth century Byzantium revived, and the Arabs were driven out of Crete, Cyprus, Antioch, Edessa and other places. In Edessa the Christian troops plundered a relic which proved to be famous, the mandylion. It portrayed on a cloth what was supposed to be the face of Christ. This relic was to become the 'Turin shroud', recently identified as a mediaeval creation.

The Abbasid empire suffered from its size and from inner turbulence. Because of its gigantic extent the provinces ruled by powerful governors could lead a life of their own. Furthermore the Sunni caliphs in Baghdad were not recognized by the various Shi'ite groups and were contested. The Ismailis, from whom the Fatimid dynasty emerged, were particularly militant. The Fatimids seized control of Egypt and Syria and left an abiding memorial by founding a capital on the Nile, Cairo (al-Qahira = the powerful).

A political sect of a special kind came into being in Persia at the end of the eleventh century. The Assassins used clandestine murder as a political means. Their name derives from their use of hashish in their cultic actions.

At its climax in the first half of the ninth century the Abbasid empire was not only a political but also a cultural great power. Baghdad was a centre of the arts and sciences. An academy continued the work of the ancient Greeks in the spheres of science (medicine, astronomy, geography, mathematics) and the humanities (philosophy).

The Abbasid caliph best known in Europe was Harun al-Rashid. But there is no historical support of claims that he was in contact with Charlemagne and even sent him a water clock as a present.

The short hey-day of Abbasid rule was followed by a protracted decline. In Baghdad and in Samara on the upper reaches of the Tigris, which for a while was a capital, the caliphs ruled only by name. The real power lay in the hands of Turkish mercenaries from Central Asia, a warrior caste which had gradually taken the place of the Arabs, who were becoming increasingly tired of war. In the middle of the eleventh century these mercenaries took over the whole power of the state and established a great new empire – the Seljuq empire. They destroyed the Armenian empire and penetrated deep into Asia Minor. Byzantium lost almost all of Anatolia and found itself confronted with a danger which was more deadly than the Arab onslaughts of the seventh and eighth centuries. The Seljuqs also seized Syria and Palestine from Byzantium and were thus in possession of the holy places of Christianity. As strictly orthodox Sunnis, they made difficulties for Christian pilgrims and thus provided the immediate occasion for the First Crusade.

The Crusades – a Christian counter-offensive

The momentous chain of events which burdened relations between Christians and Muslims over the centuries began on 27 November 1095 before the walls of the French city of Clermont. At an open-air gathering, Pope Urban II summoned the knights of Christendom to free the Christian holy places in Palestine from the hands of the 'unbelieving' Muslims. Even if we leave aside the obvious exaggerations and falsifications of contemporary reports, the Pope's speech must have been a rhetorical masterpiece. The rhetoric was immediately followed by practical implementation. A whole list of regulations relating to participation in the Recapturing of the Holy Sepulchre – thus the official title of the military organization – were already issued in Clermont. Present-day historians are clear that Jerusalem was not the only goal of the enterprise. Forty years after the official split of the church into West and East, Rome wanted to use the opportunity to settle the internal dispute over faith at the same time – by crushing the Byzantine empire.

The history of the Crusades is heroic and perverse at the same time, a web of heroic acts, cruelties, nobility and treachery, in which the Christians – if one weighs all the evil deeds against each other – were the worse. The conquest of Jerusalem in summer 1099 is typical of this. When the

Crusaders had broken through the walls of the city after a short siege, they massacred the Muslim and Jewish inhabitants without mercy. The holy places of the Temple Mount, the Dome of the Rock and the Al-Aqsa Mosque did not instil the slightest reverence in them. The German abbot Ekkehard of Aura wrote in a contemporary chronicle:

'If anyone wants to hear what happened to the enemies in the city he should hear that the victors rode up to the knees of their horses in the blood of the Saracens in Solomon's Portico and in his temple.'

After the massacre, the masters – the pride of French chivalry, with Counts Raymond of Toulouse and Godfrey of Bouillon at their head – paid homage to the Holy Sepulchre in the church only a stone's throw from the Temple Mount, and 'felt as if they were at the gates of heaven'.

A few days later the 'kingdom of Jerusalem' was proclaimed. In the course of subsequent decades it was to experience changing fortunes: military defeats by the Turkish Seljuqs and the Egyptian Fatimids were followed by victories and great territorial expansions. A struggle for power, greed for plunder, licentiousness of every kind, constant friction with Byzantium, supply problems and the inability of the knights to build up an ordered constitution, weakened the kingdom of Jerusalem. The end came when one of the most intelligent and effective rulers of the Middle Ages, Sultan Saladin, came to power in Egypt. In July 1187 he destroyed the whole military force of the Crusaders in the battle at the Horns of Hattin, two hills above Lake Genessaret. In October of the same year Saladin entered Jerusalem. He had the golden cross taken down from the cupola of the Dome of the Rock and dragged through the streets. 'The Muslims cried "Allah akbar", for joy, the

Franks shrieked in pain and dismay, and the cry was so loud and penetrating that it made the earth shake,' noted a chronicler. The interval when a Christian kingdom had been established on the soil of Palestine had lasted only eighty-eight years. Some fortified Crusader places held out longer, but when the new rulers of Egypt, the Mamluks (former Turkish mercenaries), conquered the city of Acco in 1291, the last remnant of the Crusader army in the Holy Land was destroyed. Attempts to recapture th Christian places failed.

The end of the caliphate

In the thirteenth century a weakened Seljuq empire fell victim to the rulers of an Asian empire which had its centre in the desert city of Khiva on the Aral Sea. But only a few years later this empire, too, fell to the blows of the Mongols, who under Genghis Khan created the first Asian empire – a state which at the time of its greatest extension reached from the steppes of Russia to the Sea of China. In 1258 Baghdad was conquered by the Mongols; the last Abbasid caliph fell in battle. In Egypt the caliphate was still maintained in name, until it was abolished by the Ottoman conquerors in 1517. From then on the rulers called themselves 'sultan'. This was a title which had already existed in Islam (see Saladin) but did not include the comprehensive spiritual authority of the title 'caliph'.

After the death of Genghis Khan his empire was divided. In China the Mongol conquerors became Buddhists or Confucians; in Mongolia they adopted the Lamaism of the Tibetan school; in Persia they became Muslims. In the fourteenth century Timur Lenk (Tamberlane) succeeded in reuniting the small Islamic individual kingdoms of central Asia in a great empire, but soon after Timur's death it collapsed again. One of his descendants, Babur, went from

Samarkand to India where he founded the Islamic Mogul empire. It lasted until it was broken up by the English in the middle of the nineteenth century and played an important part in the spread of Islam on the sub-continent.

The Ottoman empire – the most significant Islamic empire

Like the Seljuq empire, the Ottoman empire was a creation of Turkish peoples. The Turks came from Central Asia, where some of them still live today in an enormous area largely corresponding to the republics of Uzbekistan, Turkmenia and Azerbaijan. From the beginning of the fourteenth century the Ottoman empire spread in constant wars, above all against Byzantium, from its ancestral territory in north-west Anatolia in the direction of Europe. In the middle of the fourteenth century the Ottomans gained a foothold in the Balkans: in 1389 Serbia fell to them in the battle of the Amsel field at Kosovo. In 1453 the Ottomans conquered Constantinople and made it their capital under the name of Istanbul. The thousand-year Byzantine empire, formerly the Eastern Roman Empire, had finally gone under in a long fight to the death, left in the lurch by the West.

In Turkish history the sixteenth century is a breathtaking wave of conquests: Mesopotamia, Syria, Palestine, Egypt, Arabia including the holy places of Mecca and Medina, North Africa with the exception of the extreme west (Morocco). In 1526 the Turks defeated the Hungarians at Mohács and in 1529 were at the gates of Vienna. However, the fortifications of the city proved impregnable to the light Turkish cavalry. In 1683 the Turks applied the most modern methods of siege to the city; for them it had become the symbol of Christian Europe, and they wanted to win it over for Islam. This time they failed not because of the courage of the defenders, which in the end almost gave out, but because of the resolute common front of the West, even if it took some time to form. When on 12 September 1683 a motley force under the supreme command of Charles of Lorraine advanced against the besiegers by the precipices of the Vienna woods which had not been secured by the Turks, historically speaking that was the beginning of the end of the powerful Ottoman empire. Under the thrusts of the armoured Polish cavalry, with King John Sobieski at its head, the ring of the siege round Vienna, the capital and royal residence, was broken. As a result of the victorious campaigns of the Austrians, which were soon carried out under the supreme command of the strategic and political genius Prince Eugene of Savoy, who had immigrated from France, Turkish rule of the Balkans gradually collapsed. Wars of liberation, like that of the Greeks, and long-drawn-out military clashes with the expanding Russian empire and a general decline, meant that the Sultan's empire increasingly contracted. The domination of the Mediterranean by his fleet was lost as a result of the battle of Lepanto in 1571. The exploitation of America by the European powers led to a decline in trade in the Mediterranean, which formerly had been the centre of civilization of the Old World. The end of the Ottoman empire after its defeat in the First World War was only the finale in centuries of decline. Before Vienna and at Lepanto an era of Islamic history came to an end – the dissemination of the faith through battle and war.

The present-day distribution of Islam goes back to the waves of conquest which began in Arabia in the seventh century and ended 1,000 years later with the Turkish wars in Europe. Caliphs and sultans have disappeared with their empires, but with few exceptions (Spain and Greece), Islam has been able to maintain itself as a religion in the territories it once conquered.

4

Islam Today

The Islamic world is on the move, and to the Western world, which until the recent revolution in the former Eastern bloc had been fixed for more than four decades in the political and geographical frontiers of the European post-war order, it seems unstable and threatening. Often the radical forms of expression of the Islamic revolutions and of Islamic fundamentalism are signs of an uncertainty the roots of which are to be sought in the collapse of the Islamic sphere of power after the seventeenth century. Faced with the radical social and political change in the industrialized states and the increasing technological superiority of this First World, the Islamic countries, all of which belong to the Third World, are going through a deep identity crisis.

Re-Islamicization and fundamentalism

The separation of church and state in the Western democracies eliminates any possible political explosiveness from the fundamentalist religious tendencies which are coming into being in them. But this separation is only between one and two centuries old. European history also knows examples of the reaction of the church and political establishments to threats by fundamentalist movements in the form of a crusading mentality with fire and sword (for example in the persecutions of the Albigensians or the Hussites).

In Islam, where there is no separation of politics and religion, religious movements are always also political, and of course vice versa. The identification of religion and politics is incomprehensible to most Europeans today and seems to them to be deeply mediaeval. They forget all too easily that this union was also taken for granted in Europe for 1500 years. In 1648 the Thirty Years' War was brought to an end with the Peace of Westphalia, which guaranteed the right of every local ruler to define the religion of his subjects. Anyone who did not agree with it had to emigrate. The consequence was mass emigrations within Europe and later from Europe to America. And is it not illogical to condemn the Ayatollah in Iran, who preaches and engages in politics, while finding nothing strange in the fact that the Queen of England is the supreme head of the Church of England, the Anglican Church?

Fundamentalism is a movement back to the roots, to the beginning of the preaching or revelation of a faith. In Christianity and in Islam, both of which are 'religions of the book', this means reflection on the Bible or the Qur'an with the aim of reversing adaptations to centuries of social development. For this reason , fundamentalism and conservatism are opposites. Conservatives want to preserve the existing situation; fundamentalists want to change it. In the Islamic world the fundamentalists are often social reformers, although they seem anything but 'progressive' to Western thought.

The nineteenth century was decisive for the formation of various political ideas and concepts in the Islamic world of the present. At that time there was no mistaking the fact that the 'East' had been outstripped by the 'West' in every conceivable sphere: the Ottoman empire, which was growing increasingly weak, lost Tunis to the French (1881) and Egypt to the English (1882). India, which had at last been united as a state under the Islamic Moguls, fell to the British in 1850. The Russian Czars conquered wide areas in Islamic Central Asia (Khiva, Bukhara, Tashkent, Samarkand, Dushanbe), having previously conquered the Islamic regions of the Caucasus (e.g. Azerbaijan) and the Crimea, which was inhabited by the Muslim Tatars. It must have occurred to Muslim political thinkers that the Christian empires of Europe would incorporate the whole Islamic world as a colonial empire. Furthermore there were the wars of liberation in the Balkans, in which Christian Slavs or Greeks fought against Muslim Turks, and as a last humiliation the loss of the Islamic core territories of Bosnia and Herzegovina to Austria, whose ruler almost mockingly had 'king of Jerusalem' among his many titles.

Three thinkers from different parts of the Islamic world attempted to find an answer to the physical, spiritual and cultural domination by the West which they feared. Sayyid Ahmad Khan is called the father of reform Islam. He came from a family in Delhi which still had relations with the Mogul court, and for a while was in the service of the East India Company, whose rule over India was the prelude to incorporation into the British colonial empire. Ahmad Khan also spent some years in England. His knowledge of the West shaped his thought. He wanted to create a form of Islam which was acceptable to young people with a European education, and in this way to prevent them turning to Christianity or becoming atheists. At the same time he wanted to defend Islam against attacks by European scholars. Ahmad Khan introduced philosophical concepts from the Enlightenment, like 'nature' or 'reason', into Islam. By new interpretations he toned down Islamic concepts which caused particular offence in the West, e.g. the Holy War (jihad), polygamy, slave-owning, the harsh punishments of the Shari'a and the prohibition against levying interest. Ahmad Khan was rejected by many Islamic thinkers as being too friendly to the British, but his works were an important attempt to redefine Islam for a society which was developing in new directions.

Jamal al-Din al-Afghani worked mainly as a political activist. His aim was to make the Islamic world so strong that it was equal to the European world and thus could offer resistance to European colonialism. His creed was, 'Learn from Europe'. The Muslims were to adopt the scientific and technical achievements of the Europeans, just as in the Middle Ages the Europeans had profited from the achievements of Muslim thinkers and scientists. However, there was a need to reflect whether the new concepts were compatible with the demands of Islam. Jamal al-Din, too, interpreted the Qur'an along the lines of modern reason. Nothing in the revelations could be understood to mean that Muslims had to repudiate any technical achievements. In political terms he propagated the unity of the Islamic world against European colonialism, in the ideology of pan-Islamicism.

His pupil Muhammad Abduh was the most influential reform thinker in Islam. In his homeland, Egypt, eventually he also held offices which enabled him to put his ideas into practice. As Mufti (holder of the highest religious office in Egypt), he worked for an educational reform; here the al-Azhar University in Cairo stood at the centre of his efforts. As a member of the legislative council he argued for a legal reform, but was less successful in this area. In Egypt Abduh recognized a problem with which many Islamic states have only been confronted in our day: the gulf between the Westernized educated class and the mass of the population. Abduh wanted to bridge this gap with his teachings and reforms. The political significance that this split in the population could still have around a century after Abduh is indicated by the fall of the Shah's regime in Iran. Jamal al-Din and Abduh were both clergy. However, they wanted to achieve the renewal of Islam not by a romantic return to the roots, to original Islam, but by adopting all the spiritual achievements of Europe – including political ideas, like democracy with a Western stamp – as far as these achievements were compatible with Islam.

The counter-movement began in the 1920s and had its origin in Egypt. In 1928, Hasan al-Banna founded the Muslim Brotherhood. It developed into a mass movement which also spilled over into other Arab states. The Muslim Brothers defined re-Islamicization as a re-establishment of an Islamic constitutional and social order with Islamic legislation. Any Western influence was rejected as un-Islamic. In contrast to Saudi-Arabian fundamentalism (Wahhabism), there were marked tendencies towards social reform in the Muslim Brotherhood. In Egypt, militant members of the Muslim Brotherhood murdered President Sadat in 1981 and are still keeping his successor Mubarak on edge with attacks and revolts. In Syria they were bloodily suppressed by the Assad regime. In Jordan at the end of 1989 they won a great success in the first parliamentary elections for more than two decades.

So re-Islamicization is not a sudden or unexpected event, as it is occasionally seen to be in the West, because of one spectacular achievement, the Islamic revolution in Iran. Rather, it is a revolution with historical roots. In the following sections, re-Islamicization and fundamentalism will be discussed in specific contexts.

Islam in Europe

Mosques in Vienna, Berlin, Geneva, London, Paris, Madrid, Lisbon, Brussels and Copenhagen are an external sign that Islamic communities also exist in Western Europe. The economic boom in Western Europe sparked off the immigration of foreign workers, many of whom were and are Muslims (from former Yugoslavia and Turkey and, especially in France, from the former French colonies in North Africa).

It is estimated that there are between two and two and a half million Muslims in France – about five per cent of the population. Muslims are the largest religious community there after the Catholics, coming before Protestants and Jews. The potential for conflict was shown in 1989 by a dispute over the question whether Muslim schoolgirls, who wear a head-covering at school, were or were not offending against the non-religious status of state schools. Le Pen's ultra-right-wing National Front made political capital out of the front with xenophobic slogans, and achieved spectacular success in the polls.

However, Islam in Europe is much older than the population movements in the twentieth century. It is even much older than the Turkish conquests at the end of the Middle Ages. As early as the ninth century Muslims were living in the territory of former Yugoslavia. When the Turks conquered the Balkans in the fourteenth, fifteenth and sixteenth centuries, they came across Muslim villages in Bosnia. Ethnically only a small proportion of the Muslim population of former Yugoslavia was Turkish; the predominant majority – above all in Bosnia and Herzegovina – were Slavs.

In the nineteenth century Bosnia became a bone of contention between Croatia and Serbia. A conflict within Christianity stood in the background. The Catholic Croats wanted to play the Muslim Bosnians off against the Orthodox Serbs and vice versa. In 1878, at the Peace of Berlin which sealed the end of Turkish rule over the Balkans, Bosnia and Herzegovina were transferred to the Austro-Hungarian empire. The Austrians encouraged the nationalism of the Muslim Bosnians, who did not feel Turkish anyway. Serbia was of course furious and confirmed in its anti-Austrian attitude – one of the many factors which finally, in 1914, led to the attempt on the Crown Prince Franz Ferdinand in Sarajevo in Bosnia.

In the kingdom of Yugoslavia between the wars there was constant friction between Bosnia and Serbia. In the Second World War only a small number of the Yugoslav Muslims joined Tito's partisans, while the majority sympathized with the Grand Mufti of Jerusalem, who was well disposed to Hitler (and hated the Jews). As was usual in the occupied territories, in Yugoslavia too the SS recruited the local population to collaborate with them in their criminal acts. The people called the Bosnians in their death's-head uniform the 'Muslim SS'. Tito took his revenge on the Bosnians after his victory by persecution, expulsion and murder (there were massacres in Sarajevo and Novi Pazar). Mosques were closed or blown up. Attempts at Bosnian autonomy were set back decades. Only in 1968 did the Bosnian Muslims gain recognition of their distinct nationality – and with them the Muslim population in Croatia, Serbia and Montenegro. The Muslims in Kosovo and Macedonia were exceptions: they were given Albanian or Macedonian nationality.

The collapse of Yugoslavia plunged the Muslim nation into catastrophe. The Serbs are also waging their war against Bosnia-Herzegovina with religious undertones. Two years before the beginning of the war there was a pompous commemoration of the six hundredth anniversary of the battle of Kosovo Polje, which was a victory for the Turks. With the benevolent permission of the Serbian Communist leader Slobodan Milosevic the senior representatives of the Serbian Orthodox Church spread a kind of Christian crusader mood.

When the Serbians launched their attack, 1.6 million Muslims were living in Bosnia-Herzegovina. Within a short space of time 70% of the territory was conquered, and the Muslims were brutally expelled by force – the cynical term used by the Serbs is 'ethnic cleansing'. Hundreds of thousands of people had to leave their towns and villages. Many became the victims of terrible atrocities – massacres, mass rapes, torture in detention camps.

Mosques and houses of prayer were systematically shelled or blown up. This was also a war against a culture centuries old. The Croats also played a part. Their artillery destroyed the historical capital of Mostar and the famous sixteenth-century bridge over the Neretva, a symbol of former Ottoman rule.

The Bosnian capital Sarajevo was also a symbol. There Muslim Bosnians, Orthodox Serbs and Catholic Croats had been living peacefully together. The years-long siege of the city by the Serbs has destroyed human and cultural values as well as property and possessions. Serbian shells have been aimed at mosques, schools, theatres, museums and libraries and have left them in ruins. The Muslim community throughout the world sees what is going on in Bosnia as an attempt to exterminate a people, its culture and its religion, while Western society is looking on helpless and divided. Europe and the United Nations have failed. The suffering of the Bosnian Muslims could lead to the kind of radicalism that we have seen in the Near East for decades.

The European state with the highest proportion of Muslims in the population is Albania. Almost two-thirds of the population are Muslims. However, up to the end of the Communist dictatorship in 1991 they might not confess their faith. In 1967 the dictator Enver Hoxha had banned any practice of religion. Mosques and churches were closed, confiscated, converted to other uses or destroyed. Now that Albania has become democratic, religious structures are being rebuilt, but only slowly, since its economy is so weak. Four years after the changes, just over 100 mosques are open again. New houses of prayer and schools can only be built with the financial support of rich states like Saudi

Arabia. The human distress is so great that people are more interested in material survival than religious values.

More than 1.5 million Muslims live in Bulgaria, where they form around ten per cent of the population. They are ethnically composed of Turks, Tatars, gypsies and the so-called Pomaks, Muslims of Slavonic-Bulgarian origin, whose ancestors accepted Islam. The Pomaks are primarily the victims of a 'Bulgarization campaign', a forced assimilation which began with the replacement of Muslim forenames and family names and ended with large-scale resettlements. This policy was also applied to ethnic Turks, leading to large emigrations to Turkey. Tragically, the Pomaks do not feel themselves to be Turks, and many of the ethnic Turks of Bulgaria feel no close affinity to Turkey because their families settled in Bulgaria centuries ago. (From the end of the fourteenth century to the Congress of Berlin in 1878, present-day Bulgaria was part of the Ottoman empire.)

Life has also been problematical for Muslims in Greece. It is estimated that 150,000 of them live there; ethnically, the majority of them are Turks and so they are seen as a kind of hostile population.

A not inconsiderable number of Muslims also live in Western Europe. They came to certain states in the first half of the present century above all because of colonial links as conscripts or mercenaries: Bosnians to Austria-Hungary, Algerians and Senegalese to France, and Indians (later Pakistanis) to Great Britain. A second wave of immigration came about with the economic boom in Western Europe after the Second World War: workers from Turkey, Yugoslavia and the North African countries, students from the states in the Persian Gulf which had become prosperous because of their oil, and rather later those seeking asylum from the Middle East – Kurds, Palestinians, Lebanese, Iranians and so on. They brought a culture alien to

Europeans and their Islamic faith to countries which will probably be their final home. The peculiarity of Islam, that it regulates the life of the individual completely and fuses all Muslims into the Islamic community, brings many problems in its train – in relations with the non-Islamic environment and also within families. The different character of the Muslims, who not unnaturally are coming together even more strongly in a defensive strategy, and are putting up barriers against non-Muslims, arouses latent xenophobic feelings among the population of their host countries. Such feelings, which are usually expressed in the form of prejudices, are fed by certain personalities of the Islamic world – eccentrics like Libya's Qadaffi, and despots like Iran's Khomeini – who seem almost mediaeval, and of course Iraq's Saddam Hussein. The terrorist acts of various Arab groups have also gained the Muslims anything but sympathy, although, apart from the Lebanese Shi'ite fanatics, the terrorist organizations have no religious links, but on the contrary have tended to be far more Marxist in orientation.

The Muslims in the USA and Canada have fewer problems in living with the non-Muslim majorities. In these two countries with their classic immigration situation Muslims probably number around 21 million in all. Since the revolution in Iran the strongest contingent has come from that country. Originally Islamic immigrants came predominantly from Albania and Yugoslavia; India and Pakistan; or Egypt, Syria and Palestine.

It is worth mentioning the sect of the Black Muslims. This movement originally had little to do with Islam and its traditions. Its members prefer to be called 'African-American Muslims'. Some groups have been supported by the indefatigable Qadaffi.

The Central Asian and Caucasian empire of the Soviet Union has collapsed into many independent states. The

Muslims are the majority population everywhere except Armenia. The Tsarist empire brought Islamic peoples under its rule in several stages. The Khanates of Kazan and Astrakhan were conquered in the sixteenth century, Crimea in the eighteenth century and the trans-Caucasian countries as far as the frontiers of the Ottoman empire and Persia in the first half of the nineteenth century. In the second half of the century the Russians advanced into Central Asia and had no difficulty in occupying the Khanates of Khiva, Bukhara and Kokand.

Only a few weeks after the October Revolution the Bolshevik government issued an 'appeal to all able-bodied Muslims in Russia and in the East', signed by Lenin and Stalin. Among other things, it said: 'From now on your faith and your customs, your national and cultural institutions, are declared free and inviolable. Organize your national life free and unhindered. That is your right.' Reality proved these fine words lies. In 1917 there were 26,000 registered mosques in Russia; shortly before the end of the Soviet Union a survey indicated that there were 200 large and 1,000 small places of worship, with less than 2,000 clergy. There were two places for training clergy in the enormous territory of six republics with a majority Islamic population: a Qur'an school in Bukhara and an Islamic college in Tashkent.

It was clear to the Soviet leaders from the beginning that the ideology of atheism, which was one of the foundations of the state, could only be established by force against Islam with its totalitarian claim on believers. The Islamic courts were dissolved and the pious foundations which mainly consisted of land were nationalized, thus removing the financial basis of the religious institutions. However, the atheist Soviet state made a false assumption: Lenin and his followers believed that they could suppress Islam in the same way as they suppressed the Russian Orthodox

Church. They did not recognize that the spiritual hier-
archies and communal institutions in Islam are not
absolutely necessary for Islamic practice. The proscribed
prayers can be said even without mosques; the pilgrimage to
Mecca is compulsory only if there is a practical possibility of
carrying it out; and obeying dietary laws and commandments to fast is in any case a private matter.

So Islam was able to outlast Communist rule, and very
soon after the collapse of the Soviet Union, in the states
which subsequently came into being it could very soon
regain its former social and political status.

In Russia itself there is a large Muslim minority of about
20 million. This is organized into around 2,500 communities. By way of comparison the Russian Orthodox Church
has around 4,400 communities.

More than seventy peoples and tribes live in the
Caucasus, most of them Muslims. Before the conquest of
this area by Czarist Russia, their influence and culture was
influenced either by the Ottoman Empire or by Turkey. The
only Christian peoples in the Caucasus are the Armenians
and Georgians. Conflicts in the region display elements of a
religious struggle. Christian Armenia waged war on Muslim
Azerbaijan for the Armenian exclave of Nagorni Karabach
and as a result came under political and media fire from
Turkey and Iran: from Turkey, because the Azeris, the
inhabitants of Azerbaijan, are ethnically a Turkish people;
and from Iran, because the Azeris are Shi'ites. However,
although they have the same religion, the population of
Azerbaijan wants to have nothing to do with the mullahs'
regime in Teheran. The war waged by Russia on Chechenia
also has a religious dimension. In the last century the
mountain people put up bitter resistance against the Czarist
army for thirty years. The battle was organized by the
Murids, an Islamic brotherhood. Its most famous leader,
Imam Shmail, became a legendary figure despite his defeat.

The Afghan mujaheddin made him one of their models in the war against the Soviet aggressors.

The states which succeeded the Soviet Union in Central Asia have many problems. Politically there is the legacy of corrupt Communist local dictatorships; there is economic backwardness; and because of the Moscow population policy there is a larger or smaller Russian minority, which one day could spark off conflicts over national identities. In the quest for identity, two traditions are on offer on which the young states could build, religion and language. In the fifteenth and sixteenth centuries, when Islam was in decline in its heartlands, Central Asia was a centre of Islamic civilization. Even today the age-old oasis cities of Samarkand, Bukhara, Tashkent, Khiva and Kokand impress by their buildings and other cultural treasures. With one exception, in all five states Islamic Turkish peoples are the majority population. The exception is Tadzhikistan. The Tadzhiks are an Iranian people, akin to the people of Persia but also to what was at that time the largest population group in neighbouring Afghanistan. One day the frontiers could begin to shift – with unpredictable political consequences.

Kazakstan, Kirghizia, Uzbekistan and Turkmenistan are inhabited by Turkish peoples. However, in the course of time they have undergone diverging linguistic and cultural developments. Turkmenistan is largely desert, and a high proportion of its roughly 3.5 million inhabitants are nomads. In neighbouring Uzbekistan, around 20 million people have settled in towns and villages. Moreover the Turkmenes are more closely related to the Ottoman Turks than the Uzbeks and the Kazaks. Of course the language has also changed. Present-day Turks get on best with the Turkmenes. While Uzbekish is basically Turkish, it has been heavily influenced by Persian. Kazakish and Kirghizish are closely related. Nevertheless, all look to Turkey for help in finding national identity. Ankara is ready to help, with the ulterior motive that it can defuse potential flashpoints in the region by a sense of community. The script is a burning question. Under Soviet rule Cyrillic was commanded for all languages. Through study of the Qur'an, Arabic script is now finding a way into Central Asia, but it is not very suitable for writing down the Turkish language. Turkey has offered help with the introduction of the Latin script which it has been using since Ataturk, but for a long time this will remain a confused region.

Turkey – not an Islamic country?

From a historical perspective the Ottoman empire was the last Islamic empire. However, it differed fundamentally from all other Islamic states, because religion always played a subordinate role as a political driving force. When a last attempt was made in 1876 to prevent the collapse of the Ottoman empire, a new clause was incorporated into the constitution: the Ottoman sultan was at the same time caliph and thus 'preserver of the Islamic religion'. In this way Turkey wanted to win over the pan-Islamic movement for itself in order to be able to force through its own nationalistic interests in the face of the efforts of many territories of the empire – above all those inhabited by Arabs – to gain independence.

A historical legitimation was also found. In 1517 the Egyptian Mamluk empire was conquered by the Ottomans. The Mamluks, too, were ethnic Turks – the descendants of Turkish mercenaries. In Egypt a last offshoot of the Abbasids, who were once so powerful in Baghdad, had spent his life a caliph. According to a legend which was widespread later, he transferred the dignity of caliph to the conqueror of Egypt, the Turkish Sultan Selim I.

Constitutionally, Turkey entered world history an Islamic state. However, the situation changed fundamentally when after its defeat in the First World War it was reduced to its present limits and Mustafa Kemal Pasha, who later called himself Ataturk, seized power. Ataturk blamed Islam above all for the weakness of Turkey. He believed that necessary reforms and innovations were being prevented by the clergy. In fact it was only at the beginning of the eighteenth century that the supreme Islamic court of the Ottoman Empire allowed the building of a printing works in Istanbul. For a long time there was also opposition to building a railway line. The conclusion of the reformers (the Young Turks) was that since the fifteenth century Turkey had been a European state but because of the great influence of Islam had excluded itself from European progress. Consequently Ataturk set out to change this situation.

The republic was proclaimed in 1923, and in 1924 the caliphate was abolished and the last caliph of the country expelled. Religious instruction in all schools was progressively prohibited between 1924 and 1938. In 1925 the order of dervishes, which had played an important role in popular religion, was banned, the monasteries were closed by the state and the monks driven out. In 1926 Ataturk replaced civil law based on Islamic law with Swiss law. This also abolished the right to polygamy. Islam as a state religion was removed from the constitution, the calendar was Europeanized (which meant the adoption of the Christian calendar), Arabic script was replaced by Latin, Sunday introduced as a day of rest instead of Friday, and the cry of the muezzin was no longer allowed in Arabic but only in Turkish.

Ataturk died in 1938. The Second World War, in which Turkey remained neutral, occupied the country more markedly than the reforms. However, immediately after the war, a process began which is still going on today: most of

Ataturk's reforms were reversed. None of these reforms had changed much in the deeply rooted religion of the people. Popular religion never limited itself merely to the cult, but always had political consequences – in the primal Islamic sense.

The Islamic 'Prosperity Party' was very successful at the communal elections in 1994. Since then self-appointed Islamic guardians of virtue have been on the move, threatening women and girls in Western dress, demanding segregation by gender in public transport, attacking restaurants in which alcoholic drinks are sold, and practising a radical fundamentalism hitherto unprecedented in Turkey. Ataturk had the religious schools closed. His successors opened them again and made it possible for those who passed through such schools to go to the universities. The consequence is that an increasing number of Islamists are becoming civil servants and undermining the state administration.

The increasing fundamentalism has also accentuated the tensions between the Sunni majority and the Alevites, who make up between a quarter and a third of the Turkish population. The Alevites are Shi'ites with a strong tendency towards mysticism and an equally strong antipathy to any religious compulsion. They do not meet in mosques but in houses of prayer, and women also take part in their religious ceremonies. In 1995 fundamentalists provoked serious disturbances in an Alevite quarter of Istanbul; the political background was that the Alevites fully support Ataturk's separation of mosque and state. In officially secular Turkey the conflicts between radical Islamists on the one hand and the representatives of a secular state or religious pragmatics on the other are becoming increasingly acute.

Egypt – an Islamic country?

The question mark may seem provocative, since Egypt is of course an Islamic country. A few years after Muhammad's death it was conquered and Islamicized by the Arabs. However, a significant minority, the Copts, did not accept the Islamic faith, but remained Christian. Today the Copts number 7% of the population and have monopolies in certain professions, above all in financial matters, which have been handed over to them because of the prohibition on levying interest which is contained in the Qur'an. But in a phase of its recent history Egypt also experienced a political experiment rare in the Islamic world: Nasser's attempt to create an 'Arab socialism'. Greater social justice, redistribution of land and equal opportunities for the underprivileged were brutally forced through. However, Nasser's close foreign policy links with Moscow provoked the antagonism of the pious, who rejected Communism in principle because of its basic atheistic attitude.

Another factor justifies the question-mark after the heading above: one of the most vigorous political controversies broke out over the question of the legal system. Like many Islamic countries, in the colonial period Egypt had been given a legal system on the Western pattern. In addition, however, the Islamic law, the Shari'a, constantly existed alongside it. In recent years pressure has increased from the conservative Orthodox to include so-called Qur'anic punishments in the law book (amputation of hands and feet for theft, flogging for drinking alcohol and the death penalty for leaving the Islamic religious community). These efforts led to great tensions with the Coptic Church, which referred to the freedom of faith rooted in the constitution and the UN convention of human rights. The Coptic position provoked clashes between them and Muslim extremists.

Egypt is one of the birthplaces of the modern re-Islamicization movement, because the Muslim Brotherhood was founded there in 1928. The Muslim Brothers want to turn Egypt into an Islamic country, but are strictly against violence. Other groups are less restrained. Gama'a al-Islamya or al-Jihad are waging a war against the government. In 1981 they murdered President Sadat during a military parade, and in 1995 an attack on Sadat's successor Mubarak during a visit to the Ethiopian capital Addis Ababa failed. Attacks on tourists serve two ends: the economy of Egypt is affected by the decline in foreign visitors, and Western foreigners with their supposedly bad influence on Egyptian society are deterred. The strongholds of the Islamic extremists are in Upper Egypt. In Asyut and other cities they engage in regular battles with the police and the army. The state repels them with considerable violence. Tens of thousands of activists are arrested, whole areas of cities are sealed off and combed, and hundrds of mosques are closed. The charge of torture is constantly made at the mass trials.

The attitude of the government towards the Muslim Brotherhood is peculiar. The Brotherhood is officially banned and is accused of working with terrorists both inside and outside Egypt. But under a variety of names the Brotherhood has undertaken social work for which the state is really responsible. In the poor quarters of Cairo and other cities it offers cheap food and medicine, medical care, social welfare or legal advice. More and more people are being convinced by the slogan of the Muslim Brothers, 'Islam is the Solution'. But so far the government has refused to enter into any dialogue.

In truth the non-violent Muslim Brotherhood is a more dangerous enemy to the ruling class in Egypt than the terrorists with their guns and bombs. Only a tiny minority of the population of 60 million profits from conditions.

Politically Egypt is a stabilizing factor in the Middle East for the Western world. The peace treaty with Israel was decisive for the peace process, which by now includes almost all Israel's former opponents. Egypt played an important role as mediator in the negotiations between Israel and the PLO and in the formation of the coalition between the West and the Arabs against the Iraqi adventurer Saddam Hussein. The USA and the conservative oil states on the Gulf reward this role with billions of dollars. The stream of money will continue to flow if the government in Cairo also offers itself as a bulwark against Islamic fundamentalism.

The material distress of the people of Egypt has many causes. The prime cause is the growth in the population, with which the economy cannot keep pace. This population increases by a million every nine months. The war of the Islamic terrorists against tourists has reduced the income from foreign tourism by around one half. And of course the country still bears the heavy burden of four wars against Israel.

The Islamicization of Egyptian society is proceeding apace. The Muslim Brotherhood has a say in all the important professional associations (doctors, attorneys, technicians and students). At the al-Azhar University in Cairo, one of the most renowned centres of education in the Islamic world, young men from humble backgrounds are accepted and thus gain access to higher levels of society, which in this way are Islamicized.

Islamic banks and investment organizations have become an economic power factor. The government is vainly attempting to bring them under its control. These Islamic banks interpret Muhammad's prohibition against interest as 'prohibition against excessive interest' – with the emphasis on the excessive. They are flourishing throughout the Islamic world. In Egypt, however, they are a challenge to the state, to which they offer an alternative.

The Austrian political theorist Fadil Rasoul, born a Kurd, who was murdered in Vienna in 1989 together with Ghassemlou, the Kurdish leader, probably by the Iranian secret service, regards the development of Egypt as logical: 'It seems almost natural for it to link up once more with its Islamic roots, when one remembers that in the collective memory of Egyptian society the Western model of Reform ('left-wing' Nasserism and 'liberal' Sadatism) were noted and assessed as failures.'

North Africa (The Maghreb)

During the course of the seventh and eighth centuries, the Islamic Arab armies had advanced from the Nile Delta to the Atlantic. As North Africa is not a uniform area of settlement and even the fertile regions on the Mediterranean coast are separated by deserts, no unitary state developed. Even the Ottoman empire could only establish its rule superficially in what – from the perspective of Istanbul – was a remote area. The influence of Europe constantly kept making itself felt, above all from the nineteenth century on, when the area was colonized (by Spain, France and finally Italy).

Morocco, geographically the westernmost of the Maghreb states, most clearly detached itself from the supremacy of Istanbul. For centuries the Arab princes who resided in cities like Rabat, Fez or Marrakesh had close associations with the Muslim rulers of Spain. When after their defeat in 1492 the Moors were confronted with the choice of going over to Christianity (according to Islamic law a crime punishable by death) or emigrating, they emigrated in hordes, along with the Spanish Jews who were facing a similar threat, over the Straits of Gibraltar to Morocco. By 1912 the Sultan of Morocco had lost so much power, above all economically, that France and Spain occupied the country and divided it between them. After the end of the Second World War the independence movement which came into being in the 1930s (Istiqlal) at first provoked repressions from the power supervising the protectorate (France), but in 1956 achieved a French withdrawal.

King Hassan II, who has ruled since 1961, is the supreme secular and spiritual head ('Ruler of the faithful') of Morocco. The conflicts between the Europeanized upper class and the people are growing deeper. The fundamentalist 'right', which is increasingly gaining influence, is particularly dangerous. The situation is exacerbated by the sorry economic situation of the country, caused above all by the war in what was once the Spanish colony of West Sahara.

Tunisia, since the sixteenth century a province of the Ottoman empire, was made a French protectorate around thirty years earlier than Morocco, and similarly gained its independence in 1956. A year later, the leader of the independence movement, Habib Bourgiba, deposed the last Bey and declared Tunisia a republic. Bourgiba's party, the Socialist Destour Party, was renamed the 'Constitutional Democratic Assembly' after Bourgiba's deposition in 1987 by the then president, Ben Ali. However, the party does not offer a definitive ideological programme. While the state religion of Tunisia is Islam, the state calls itself secular. Sunday is the weekly holiday, and the fast of Ramadan is not an obligation. Alcohol is not forbidden. A fundamentalist movement has been fighting against this 'evil' and gained a great many votes in the elections in 1989. Since 1978 social unrest has continually shaken the country and poses a danger to its orientation, which is Western in every respect. From 1982 until relatively recently Tunis was the headquarters of Yassir Arafat's PLO. In foreign policy Tunisia plays a mediating role between the Islamic and the Western world.

The third Maghreb state, Algeria, has taken quite a
different direction. From 1830, French immigrants colonized the land both economically and politically. France
waged a bloody and sometimes very dirty colonial war
over Algeria between 1954 and 1962 which it took the
authority of Charles de Gaulle to end. Independent
Algeria was developed as a 'socialist' state by its political
leaders Ben Bella and Boumédienne and praised as a
model for the Third World. But even the great resources
of natural oil and gas could not prevent the economic
ruin of the country. The Algerian model failed as a result
of the wrong kind of investment, like the attempt to build
up heavy industry, the corruption of the regime, and not
least the rapid growth in population. It has been
calculated that within thirty years the number of inhabitants will double to 50 million. More than one third
of the population is under twenty-five and has no future
prospects. Against this background extremism flourishes.
At the end of 1991 the regime of the FLN unity party
allowed free parliamentary elections for the first time.
When the victtory of the radical Islamic Salvation Front
(FIS) looked likely, the military, in whose hands power
really was, stopped the election. The Salvation Front was
banned and its leaders imprisoned. Since then there has
been a state of war in Algeria. The radical Islamists are
shoorting and bombing, rioting against the police and the
army, and murdering local politicians and intellectuals
and foreign experts, journalists and diplomats. The government is fighting the terror with mass arrests, napalm
and lynch law. France is supporting the Algerian authorities because it fears an unpredictable state on the other
side of the Mediterranean, prepared to use violence. The
FIS leaders in prison or exile no longer have any influence
on the party. The commandos have taken over and are
engaged in radical action.

Islam in the three Maghreb states of Morocco, Tunisia and Algeria is stamped by a marked contrast between the 'popular Islam' of the broad masses and the 'state Islam' of the small ruling classes. Popular Islam is characterized by customs and views which in part go back to the time of Roman rule over the province of Africa. Agricultural customs and prayers for rain are typical fertility rites of an agrarian population. A cult which is similarly built on the rhythm of the agricultural year consists in a new year festival and a midsummer festival, neither of which is governed by the Islamic lunar calendar but by the Julian solar calendar of the Romans. The worship of personified demons; ecstasy and trances; miracle healers, mystics and pilgrimages are part of popular Islam. Amulets as protection against the 'evil eye' are worn on girdles, and healing amulets are inscribed with ink made from the burnt wool of a sacrificial lamb, dissolved in water and drunk against all kind of illnesses. The performance of these practices is often associated with special sacred shrines which frequently specialize in particular problems: family and sexual, medical, the treatment of nervous disorders caused by environmental influences. These practices of popular Islam with their psychosomatic effects have moved from the country into the big city slums as a result of the flight from the land. They are reluctantly tolerated by the governments of the three Maghreb states, because they contribute towards keeping the people quiet. However, their anarchic tendencies are not particularly welcome to the technocrats in power and the official Islamic hierarchy.

For a period of many centuries Libya shared the history of the Maghreb states, but in the twentieth century it underwent a different development. When after an agreement with England and France, Italian troops landed in Libya in 1911, they met with vigorous resistance. However, it was not the soldiers of the distant sultan in Istanbul who were fighting, but the indigenous Arab population. The resistance was organized by an Islamic sect, the Sanussiya Brotherhood. It is named after its founder and strives for the mystical union of believers with the Prophet Muhammad. The first Sanussiya monastery in present-day Libya came into being in 1842. The Sanussiya monasteries were religious centres with a markedly puritanical orientation. Their principles of prayer and work were similar to those of the Christian Benedictine order. Like the monastic orders of mediaeval Christianity, they acted as colonizers, since they involved the Bedouins in working the land.

At first the Italians could establish themselves only in the coastal cities, but after the Fascists seized power they made new efforts to conquer the whole of Libya. They eventually succeeded, despite the hard resistance of the Sanussiya, whose legitimate ruler, later to become King Idris, lived as a child in exile in Egypt – but only in 1931. Twelve years later Mussolini's soldiers had to leave the country, when with Rommel's Afrika Korps they lost the desert war against the British. After the war Libya was administered from Great Britain and in 1951 was given its independence. King Idris, the descendant of the founder of the order, took power. In 1969 he was deposed by a military coup, the leader of which was the twenty-seven year old colonel Muammar al-Qadaffi.

The slogan of the monarchy, 'God – King – Fatherland', was replaced by 'Freedom – Socialism – Unity'. Qadaffi's aim is the social transformation of the whole world through a socialist revolutionary process. Islam also plays an important role in this. This was expressed most clearly in the reforms of penal law which increasingly introduced Qur'anic punishments like stoning, amputation of hands and flogging.

Qadaffi explained his ideas in numerous speeches, and gave them written form in *The Green Book*. In their final version they are officially called the 'Third Universal Theory'. Qadaffi recognizes the Qur'an as the foundation of the social system (that is also Point 2 of the 'Quasi-Constitution' of Libya, which has four points), and speaks in socialist terms of revolutionary masses, but rejects Communism as radically as capitalism. By Western definition the 'Arabic Libyan Socialist Popular Jamahiriya' – thus the official name of the country – is a military dictatorship with basic democratic institutions.

The unpredictable Qadaffi came into conflict not only politically with the USA and practically all of the West – above all through his vigorous support of many terrorist organizations – but also with the Islamic authorities. In 1978 he spoke out radically against traditional Sunni teaching and Sunni law, polemically attacked the Hadith, the tradition of the acts of Muhammad, condemned the veneration of holy men and described the fixing of the beginning of Muslim chronology to the hijra as pagan. Qadaffi wants to introduce the day of Muhammad's death as the first day of the Muslim calendar. In so doing he has drawn down upon himself the wrath of many Islamic scholars, who accuse him of slander, heresy and unbelief. There is no central authority for questions of faith in Islam, like the Pope in the Catholic Church. The influential 'League of the Islamic World', the most important non-state international Islamic organization, called on Qadaffi to repent of his 'heresies' publicly, which of course he did not do.

Despite Qadaffi's caprices, the political situation in Libya is relatively stable, since the revenue from oil production has also benefitted the people. But like so many Arab countries, Libya, too, has suffered from the fall in oil prices and that could produce tensions and unrest.

Iran – an Islamic republic

The old empire of Persia, for centuries a rival of the Greeks, the Romans and the Byzantines, was Islamicized as early as the seventh century. The proclamation of the twelver Shi'a as the state religion in the sixteenth century was of great historical importance. It gave Iran a special position in the Islamic world. Sunnis lived in the neighbouring regions, as they still do. Because of the aggressive character of the Shi'a, this necessarily led to tensions and conflicts. On the other hand an Iranian national feeling could develop, based not only on the ethnic distinction between the Indo-Iranian tribes of Persia and the Arabs and Turks of neighbouring regions, but also on religion, which plays such an important role in the Islamic world. The national pride of the Iranians, nourished by the awareness that they had not been conquered either by the Ottoman empire or by the colonial powers of England and Russia, governed the policy both of Shah Muhammad Reza Pahkevi and of Ayatollah Khomeini.

Since the introduction of Shi'a as the state religion, the Shi'ite clergy have had great social influence and economic power in Iran. That is connected with the functions of the clergy, which are by no means limited to prayer and worship. Property is entrusted to the mullah to administer; he looks after widows and orphans and the weakest members of society; he is a kind of notary for authenticating documents of all kinds; he collects and administers monetary donations and supplies institutions like mosques and religious schools with their resources. Of course the Shi'ite clergy also supervise the observance of the Islamic law.

The conflict of the mullahs with Shah Reza was pre-programmed. The Shah led anything but the life of a pious Muslim, although he occasionally appeared in mosques.

The land reform which he introduced threatened an important source of clergy income. His reform of family law, which among other things made divorce more difficult for husbands, was as much regarded as an offence against Islamic law as was the introduction of active and passive suffrage for women in 1962. A year later the mullahs staged revolts in a number of cities; one of the clergy, Ayatollah Khomeini, had a particularly high profile here. Thereupon he was banished. In exile in Turkey, later in Iraq and finally in France, he had time to work out his radical concept of an Islamic republic.

In the meantime Shah Reza got on with making Iran a secular state with Western values. His pattern of harking back to ancient pre-Islamic Persia was intended to limit the social influence of the Shi'ite clergy. Reza's pompous coronation as Shah in 1967, the even more pompous festival to celebrate 2,500 years of Persia, and the life of luxury led by the ruling class, together with the powerful military armament financed by the billions of dollars earned through oil, were accompanied with rising dissatisfaction on the part of the lower classes. The result was increasingly brutal repression by the police and the secret police (Savak). Resistance became articulate above all in the mosques. In 1978 the Shah ordered troops to open fire on demonstrators in Teheran. That was too much for the opposition. The constitutional form of the monarchy was to fall along with the hated Shah. After the revolution the recipe for a new order was ready: Khomeini's Islamic republic.

Within a year Khomeini achieved his goal: in January the Shah and his family fled abroad, in February the seventy-seven year old Khomeini returned in triumph from exile in Paris to Teheran, and in December the new constitution was accepted in a referendum.

The constitution not only establishes Iran as an 'Islamic republic', the state religion of which is Islam, but also emphasizes the leading role of the clergy in all state institutions. A 'Council of Guardians' made up of twelve clergy ensures that none of the laws passed by Parliament offends against Islamic law. No sphere of private or public life, including politics, economic, justice, the army and culture, may rest on anything but an Islamic foundation. In 1988 it was possible to negotiate a cease-fire in the war with Iraq, although Khomeini had declared this war, which broke out in 1980 as a result of an Iraqi attack, a jihad, i.e. a holy war.

The central point of the Constitution is Article Five:

'During the absence of the exalted twelfth imam – may God grant that he come soon – government in the Islamic Republic and authority to govern the affairs of the Islamic community is to lie with a man learned in the law who is just, god-fearing, informed about the needs of the time, bold and capable of leadership, and who is recognized and confirmed as Islamic leader by the majority of the population. If no Islamic legal authority finds such a majority, government is to be exercised by a governing council of Islamic authorities on the law who fulfil the above conditions.'

The Islamic Republic made a complete U-turn from the course on which Shah Reza had embarked. Islamic punishments were introduced, and participation in Friday prayer was made compulsory; sexual intercourse outside marriage became a criminal offence, and women were compelled to veil their bodies completely, apart from face and hands. In schools and in public places segregation of the sexes was introduced, along with much else. A special apparatus ensured by force the observance of the many commandments and prohibitions. However, the 'Revolutionary Guard' (Pasdaran) soon had to exchange their pleasant life, in which they were mainly occupied with maltreating women who had offended against the laws on dress, for service in the Iran-Iraq war.

In the name of Islam, Ayatollah Khomeini at times proceeded against all opposition, real or supposed, in as brutal and bloody way as the Shah before him. Khomeini owed the fact that the stability of his rule was nevertheless preserved until the end of his life (1989) not only to the respect he enjoyed among the people, but also to a political opponent whom he described with a great many derogatory epithets ('Satan', 'Zionist agent' and so on): the Iraqi President Sadam Hussein. Saddam Hussein believed that his neighbour, preoccupied with bloody purges in its domestic affairs, could not oppose armed action to settle an old frontier dispute in in the Shatt al-Arab and intervened. But the war proved to be a factor which bound Iranian society together, especially as it soon developed into a regular blood cult and martyr cult, of the type so characteristic of the Shi'ite tendency. When Khomeini declared the war a jihad, he was stating that those who fell on the Iranian side went straight to paradise. The simple soldiers, who became younger and younger as the war dragged on, had plastic 'keys to paradise' hung round their necks to make them even more willing cannon-fodder. The Iranian child soldiers throwing themselves against the tanks and barrages of the Iraqis are among the most fearful images of this war.

Iranian sentiment was further bolstered by the fact that almost all the Arab states took the side of Iraq (Syria and Libya were the exceptions). The main reason for this was the fear of an export of the Iranian revolution, which was constantly threatened by Khomeini. The fanatical religious state on the other side of the Gulf posed a serious threat above all to Saudi Arabia, whose state religion (Wahhabi) had already been in the most marked contrast to the Iranian Shi'a for more than 150 years. In addition there was the international situation: having lost the Shah of Iran as the pillar of its influence in this oil-producing region which was so important for it and the whole of the West, the USA put Saudi Arabia in the role. In fact Iran made two attempts to destabilize the Saudi regime by specially trained 'pilgrims to Mecca'.

However, Lebanon, torn apart by a civil war, was the most important place for the importation of the Iranian revolution. Iranian terrorists established themselves in Baalbek with the aim of spreading Khomeini's revolution throughout the country and in this way threatening Israel. The 'liberation' of Jerusalem always played a special role in Khomeini's rhetoric. The complete splitting of Lebanon, in which the Iranian revolutionaries could not even rely on their numerous Shi'ite fellow believers, brought these plans to grief.

Shortly before his death, Khomeini once again attracted world-wide attention with a so-called fatwa, an Islamic judicial statement. This fatwa was directed against Salman Rushdie, a writer who had been born in India but who lived in England. Khomeini accused him of having insulted Islam in his book *The Satanic Verses*. As Rushdie had been born a Muslim, he had thus committed heresy (zandaqa). According to Islamic law this carries the death penalty. And Rushdie cannot escape this pronouncement even by abjuring his faith, since to leave the Islamic community is also punishable by death. In his fatwa Khomeini called on all Muslims to carry out the judgment. In addition he put a price of one million dollars on Rushdie's head.

In fact Rushdie's book does contain some passages which could hurt the religious feelings of Muslims. This is even true of the title. *The Satanic Verses* refers to a passage in the Qur'an which was deleted from the final version because according to valid tradition it was given to the Prophet by Satan. In reality, this may have been a compromise on the part of Muhammad in an early phase of his activity, when he also allowed the worship of the pre-Islamic deities Lat, Uzzah and Manat in the Ka'ba. This interpretation is vigorously disputed by official Islam. Moreover in his book Rushdie presents the Prophet himself under the almost transparent pseudonym of 'Mahound'. 'Mahound' was used as a taunt name by the British colonial rulers in Islamic India. In Rushdie's book prostitutes bear the names of Muhammad's wives.

Despite a heated anti-Rushdie mood in a large part of the Islamic world, which became hysterical, there were Islamic scholars who, while rejecting the book in principle, kept a clear head. The Mufti of Cairo, a scholar of the renowned al-Azhar University in Cairo, issued his own fatwa which stated that Rushdie could not be proclaimed guilty without a trial. Moreover a trial in the absence of the accused was invalid. And even if the death sentence was legitimately pronounced, the verdict could be carried out only by the competent Islamic authorities. The Rushdie affair clearly shows how deep is the gulf between Western and Islamic thought. Since for Muslims religion is not a private matter, 'Muslims' felt collectively insulted and attacked by Rushdie. They simply could not understand that people in the West were reacting sensitively to a call for the murder of a Muslim author by one of the highest spiritual and political leaders in the Islamic world. Rushdie went underground; the EC states were on the verge of breaking off diplomatic relationships with Iran. Those who – in contrast to the vast majority of protesters – have in fact read *The Satanic Verses* regard the reactions to a confused and confusing book by an extreme egocentric as exaggerated. They do not reflect that in his judgment the Iranian Ayatollah was not thinking of literary criticism. He had not read the book.

The heat against Rushdie was politically perhaps an attempt to give new impetus to the exhausted Islamic revolution. The cease-fire in the Iran-Iraq war damaged

Teheran's image. All offers of the aggressor Iraq to negotiate, when it was clear that its offensive had got bogged
down, were rejected by Iran because it wanted to overthrow
the regime of the 'Satan Saddam Hussein' in Baghdad. But
Iran did not succeed here, any more than it succeeded in
destabilizing the hated Saud regime on the other side of the
Gulf or in exporting the Islamic revolution to other
countries. The death of Khomeini, who enjoyed high esteem
as a scholar even in those parts of the Islamic world which
rejected him as a politician, probably meant the end of this
Islamic revolution. But its underlying idea – rejection of the
West, of modernism, materialism, atheism and other trends
of the time – lives on. Coupled with Shi'ite fanaticism and
the specific Shi'ite disposition towards martyrdom, this
contains a latent potential for tensions.

Saudi Arabia – a sect becomes a state

The history of the Saudi Arabian state begins in the year
1745. At that time the religious reformer Muhammad ibn
Abd al-Wahhab made a treaty with the tribal leader
Muhammad ibn Saud. The ruler committed himself to
disseminating the puritanical teachings of Wahhab. In the
course of the subsequent campaigns, which were defined as
holy war (jihad), the Sauds advanced in the direction of
Mesopotamia, captured the city of Kerbala, which was holy
to the Shi'ites, killed all the inhabitants and destroyed one of
the greatest Shi'ite sanctuaries, the tomb of the third imam,
Husain, the grandson of the Prophet. A little later Mecca
and Medina also fell into the hands of the Wahhabis, where
they wrought similar destruction on age-old Islamic tombs.
The Wahhabis reject any form of the cult which is not – like
prayers and fasting – explicitly mentioned in the Qur'an.
This especially applies to the cult of the saints and martyrs,
which has become particularly dear to the Shi'ites. Today

even members of the Saudi royal family are buried in anonymous tombs somewhere in the desert.

The first Saudi Arabian kingdom was destroyed by the Turks in 1818, because with their fanatical ideology of conquest the Wahhabis had become troublesome to the Sultan in Istanbul. A second attempt to found a Wahhabi state took place in 1824 and ended in 1891 with the banishment of the Saud family to Kuwait.

The history of the present kingdom of Saudi Arabia begins in 1902 with the conquest of Riyadh by Ibn Saud, who was twenty at the time. From Riyadh, Ibn Saud gradually won back the former kingdom by military, diplomatic and missionary means. The outbreak of the First World War was a stroke of luck for him, because the British allied themselves with the Bedouin tribes in order to threaten Turkey, which was fighting on the side of Germany and Austria-Hungary, on its south-eastern flank. After the end of the war, Ibn Saud conquered further areas on the Arabian peninsula, above all the Hejaz with the holy cities of Mecca and Medina. That concluded the expansive phase of Saudi Arabian history, for any further attempt to gain new territories would have led to conflict with the dominant powers in the Middle East, Great Britain and France. A last opponent to Ibn Saud arose out of his own ranks. Ibn Saud had provoked the Ikhwan movement. This stood for the complete unity of life and religion. Hundreds of settlements were established, which served as military and missionary centres and also as centres for the agricultural development of the surrounding countryside. An important effect of this was that Ibn Saud had at his disposal a standing army of Muslim warriors in the Bedouins who had become sedentary. The Ikhwan were not content with what had been achieved and invaded Iraq and Transjordan. Moreover with religious zeal they attacked the introduction of 'un-Islamic' innovations like cars, telephones and telegraphs. Ibn Saud finally took military action against them and in 1930 eventually forced them to capitulate. The country took the name of Saudi Arabia in 1932 and Ibn Saud became its first king.

Religious zeal still characterizes the Saudi Arabian society at a time of wealth, as it did when oil was still not an economic factor and the desert land was poor. A kind of religious police, the 'Mutatawa', controls the observance of the Wahhabi commandments and prohibitions: for example complete veiling of women, the closing of business during times of prayer, the observance of the commandments to fast and the prohibition of alcohol and nicotine. The attitude of the Islamic lawyers is equally strict. The so-called Qur'anic penalties are regularly inflicted in Saudi Arabia: adulterers are killed, thieves have a hand amputated, those guilty of drinking alcohol are flogged. Islamic law applies equally to non-Muslim foreigners. Christians are forbidden to practise their religion publicly or to engage in missionary activities. In 1989 the last remnants of ancient Christian churches in the Asir mountains were demolished.

There is a certain irony in the fact that so puritanical a regime as that of the Saudi Wahhabis is the guardian of the holiest places of Islam. The Iranian Shi'ites state that the Saudi rule over Mecca and Medina is illegitimate. Moreover the Saudi royal family acts with an iron fist against any attempt at destablization. The roughly 400,000 Shi'ites in the country – ten per cent of the population as a whole – are watched suspiciously and socially segregated. In 1979 rebels established themselves in the Great Mosque in Mecca. They were removed with the help of a French anti-terrorist unit. Legal authorities have issued a fatwa which forbids the bearing of any weapon in the sacred precincts. In 1987 Iranian pilgrims caused unrest in Mecca, by declaring the pilgrimage a political demonstration and appealing to

Khomeini. The Saudi Arabian police were prepared for this and opened fire. The list of Shi'ite martyrs grew longer, and the mullahs in Teheran swore vengeance, but the pilgrimages went on peacefully the next year. Riyadh rigorously limited the number of travel permits for Iranian pilgrims.

Saudi Arabia is a prime example of the difficulties in the process of modernizing an Islamic country. The prosperity, indeed luxury, in which almost the whole population lives is hard to reconcile with the Islamic traditions. The Bedouins, who have become sedentary, strenuously try to retain their roots, which includes life in the desert. Saudi Arabian princes travel from the cities with air-conditioned estate cars and put up tents in the desert – equipped with a generator for the air-conditioning and a video recorder. The sparsely-populated land has to import foreign workers who must live in ghettos because they are not trusted. Even if they have been to school, there is hardly any profession that women can engage in. They are not even allowed to drive cars. For all its pro-Western foreign policy, the Islamic state of Saudi Arabia, which is especially puritanical and fundamental in its spiritual orientation, rejects all Western values just as firmly as the state which the West so castigated, the state which Ayatollah Khomeini created out of pro-Western Iran.

Syria – Iraq – Jordan – Israel

Syria is an Islamic country, but not an Islamic state. A very religious population has a political government which is critical of Islam. 70% of the Syrian population are Sunni Muslims. In addition to about 12 per cent of Christians, in Syria there is a series of Islamic sects which are to be classified as Shi'ites, like the Alawis, the Ismailis and the Druze. Since 1963 the ruling party has been the Ba'ath party, which was founded by Michel Aflaq and for that very reason comes up against mistrust from the Muslim population. Ideologically the Ba'ath party has replaced Islam with an Arab nationalism. Certainly Islam is recognized as part of a fundamental Arabism, but at the same time it is also regarded as one of the causes of Arab decline. Since 1970 Syria has been ruled by the Alawi dictator Hafiz al-Assad. He turned the population against him when he removed the clause in the constitution that the president of the state had to be a Muslim. Riots in some cities were put down with much bloodshed. Since then resistance has made itself felt in the form of bombings. The regime blames the banned Muslim Brotherhood for the attacks.

In Iraq, the Ba'ath party has been in power since 1968. However, that did not prevent Syria from taking sides with Iran in the Iran-Iraq war and supporting Teheran in every conceivable way. Thus for example Israeli transport planes were allowed to overfly the country to deliver spare parts to Iran for the weapons supplied by the USA. The majority of the population of Iraq are Shi'ites (55 per cent), but they have played a subordinate role in government and administration since the days of the Ottoman empire. The Iraq Ba'ath party is in favour of a clear separation between politics and religion and in so doing is taking over a Western concept. The Shi'ites, to whom this way of thinking is completely alien, therefore represent a potential for unrest. The regime of Saddam Hussein (who has been state president and party leader since 1979) keeps them down with brutal suppression. In 1980 20,000 Shi'ites were banished. The head of the Shi'ite community was accused of having collaborated with Khomeini, condemned to death and executed. During the Iraq-Iran war, which began in 1980 with an Iraqi attack on Iran, the Iraqi Sh'iites did not offer any opposition to the government. Saddam Hussein, who is the subject of a great personality cult, developed the custom of visiting mosques regularly to demonstrate Muslim piety.

Despite turbulent periods in its history, Jordan is an element of stability in the Middle East. This is above all thanks to King Hussein. He traces his descent from the Hashemites and is thus a descendant of Muhammad. The Hashemites were for centuries guardians of the holy places of Mecca and Medina, but were exiled by Ibn Saud in 1925 and were given the desert area east of the Jordan – Transjordan – by the British. In parallel to the foundation of the state of Israel in 1948, this became the kingdom of Jordan. In 1967 the Old City of Jerusalem with the Dome of the Rock and the al-Aksa Mosque, along with all the territory west of the Jordan, was lost to Israel. In 1994 the states of Israel and Jordan made peace. In Jordan the process of democratization has also brought Islamic parties into parliament, but politically they are very moderate.

The foundation stone of a Palestinian state was laid in 1993 by the reciprocal recognition of Israel and the most important representative organization of the Palestinians, the Palestine Liberation Organization (PLO), under its president, Yasser Arafat. This was preceded by a campaign of civil disobedience (Intifada) lasting for decades, with occasional terrorist actions launched by radical Palestinians. The focal point of extremist forces is the 'Islamic Resistance Movement' (abbreviated as 'Hamas'). This is a now militant branch of the Egyptian Muslim Brotherhood in the Gaza strip, a region which was Egyptian until 1967 and is now under Palestinian self-rule. Hamas fanatics are attempting to torpedo the peace process with suicide attacks in Israel. The aim of Hamas is the destruction of Israel and the foundation of an Islamic state of Palestine.

Islam in Asia

From a purely geographical perspective, Islam is an Asian religion, since the Arabian Peninsula is part of the great continent of Asia. However, historically and politically this region, which is open towards the Mediterranean, cannot be called Asian. At a very early stage Islam spread in waves of conquest to Persia and Asia Minor, to the Caucasus and the areas of Central Asia north of Persia lying beyond the Oxus. The fact that the Mongols for the most part did not accept Islam is of historical significance. As a result there was no pressure on the most important civilization in Asia – China – to adopt this religion with its claim to totality and its expansionist drive.

The Muslim minority in China numbers about 20 million. Apart from a closed area of settlement in the north-western province of Xinjiang, they live in small groups. However, the isolated Muslim communities have preserved their faith and customs for centuries. Even the brutal persecution by the Red Guards during the Cultural Revolution could not change this attitude. Ethnically, most of the Muslims are Turkish, and this can cause tension with the Chinese. In 1989 the Beijing government proclaimed some measures aimed at calming the budding Muslim nationalism. These included the creation of restaurants which followed the Qur'an in their preparation of food, and the availability of food that believing Muslims could eat in trains and plains and on ships. The Muslims in China played a political role during the Chinese-Soviet conflict. At the end of the 1950s a Muslim organization was founded in Xinjiang with massive support from Moscow in money, arms and training. In 1958 the Muslims even proclaimed an Uigurian Republic. Their fight was against the massive Sinification policy of Mao Tse-Tung and had nothing to do with the ideological conflict between the two Communist systems.

Indonesia is the largest Islamic nation in the world. About 80 per cent of the more than 150 million Indonesians are Muslims. But Indonesia is not an Islamic state. Certainly, on the basis of the constitution, every citizen has to believe in the 'one and only God', but five religions – Islam, Hinduism, Buddhism, Catholicism and Protestantism – are recognized as having equal rights. The government may not interfere in the religious life of citizens. Political tensions keep arising from the demand of the Islamic parties for the recognition of Islamic law (the Shari'a) as the basis of the state.

By contrast, in Malaysia Islam is a state religion. However, as the Shari'a is not the basis of legislation, even Malaysia cannot be designated as an Islamic state.

There are problems with a Muslim minority in the Philippines. In the south of this widespread group of islands the Spaniards who colonized the country in the sixteenth century found Muslim sultanates on Mindanao and the islands of the Sulu archipelago. The Spaniards waged war for more than 300 years against the Filipino Muslims, whom they called 'Moros' (after the Moors, the Islamic conquerors of Spain). The minority conflict outlasted Spanish colonial rule. The United States, the power with the mandate, also had difficulties, as did the government in Manila after independence in 1946. The Moros called for the foundation of an 'Islamic Republic of Mindanao and Sulu', thus giving President Marcos a pretext to impose martial law on the whole country. The civil war on Mindanao was continued even after the revolution and the accession of President Corazon Aquino to office.

One of the most important countries in the Islamic world is Pakistan, an 'artificial state' which was founded as a state for the Muslims on the sub-continent when the British colony of India was partitioned in 1947. This so to speak pre-programmed problems, since the new state consisted of two parts (East Pakistan and West Pakistan) separated by the whole width of the sub-continent. This state had been decided on because there are Muslim majority populations in both West and East – though they do not belong together ethnically. After a bloody civil war in which India eventually intervened, East Pakistan became independent under the name Bangladesh.

Islam in Pakistan is split into countless sects. About 75 per cent of the population are nominally Sunnis. In addition there are Ismailis split into three sects, who are only half-recognized by orthodox Muslims because of their close connections with Hinduism. The Ismailis have their own mosques, pray only three times a day, read the Qur'an in Gujarati rather than Arabic and allow their women to go out in public without veils. The Ahmadis are not recognized as Muslims at all, although their rites are far more orthodox than the Ismailis.

Islam in Pakistan is stamped above all by the marked contrasts between the 'official church' and the 'popular church'. Mysticism, superstition and an extreme veneration of holy men play a major role among the people. Several pilgrimages to the tomb of a saint are equated with a pilgrimage to Mecca. A local saint called Qalandar first became the object of a popular song, then the hero of a tremendously popular hit, and finally the focal point of a dance cult. The highly controversial Islamicization campaign under the dictator Zia ul-Haq clearly ran out of steam after his death in 1988, and the fact that a woman (Benazir Bhutto) could become prime minister clearly shows that Islam in Pakistan is markedly different from Islam in Iran or Saudi Arabia.

In neighbouring Afghanistan a very fundamentalist Islam was the bond which united the warlike tribes of the country against the Soviet invasion. When the last Soviet troops withdrew after ten years of war, the internal Afghan conflicts broke out again. Popular groups like the Tadjiks or Pashtuns are fighting for control. Islamic fanatics like the Taliban want to impose their mediaeval world-view with force of arms.

Islam in Africa

It is estimated that around 100 million Muslims live in Black Africa, i.e. all the African states with the exception of the five Mediterranean countries Egypt, Libya, Tunisia, Algeria and Morocco. In some states (e.g. Mauritania or Somalia), almost the whole population is Muslim. Other states are predominantly Muslim or have larger or smaller Muslim minorities, but regionally these often form the majority population. Africa cannot be seen as a unity either historically or politically. That is also reflected in the distribution of Islam.

The first contacts with Islam took place on the shores of the Indian ocean. Even before Muhammad there were trade relations between Arabia and the territories of the present-day states of Ethiopia, Eritrea or Somalia. Islam slowly penetrated the interior of Africa following the Arab traders – including the slave traders. Except for Christian Ethiopia, where there was also a large Jewish community (the Falashas), the Muslims everywhere encountered nature religions of very different kinds. Islam established itself above all because of the social prestige associated with the acceptance of the faith. The Muslims were regarded as the bearers of a higher culture which was documented simply by the fact that a book – the Qur'an – played a dominant role in their worship.

Muslims as a social group had little influence on the liberation and decolonization movements of the last few decades. The foundation of an 'Islamic state', i.e. a state with the Shari'a as the basis of its legislation, was not even considered in those countries in which Muslims were the majority population.

The dissemination of Islam in black Africa is often merely a matter of statistics, because the traditional tribal religions continued to exist under a thin veneer of Islam.

For centuries Islam in Africa was inseparably associated with the name of one city: Timbuktu. This crossroads of old caravan routes, on the river Niger, was a trading place for salt, grain, dates, gold and slaves, and was also a cultural and spiritual centre of the continent.

In its heyday, Timbuktu had a university and 180 Qur'an schools, and was famous for 'its political freedoms, permanent institutions, purity of customs, toleration of the poor and strangers and its cultivation of the sciences', as a contemporary wrote. But the city began to decline in the sixteenth century, and today it is an insignificant place in the state of Mali, waging a hopeless war against the desert, which is approaching the city from all sides.

1,400 years after its origin, Islam, the world religion, is also a political factor – in contrast to the other world religions. Christianity or Buddhism do not make this comprehensive claim to the permeation of private and public life. The Islamic world is not a bloc, but despite all the internal tensions, crises and conflicts it demonstrates a sense of community extending beyond economic or political interests. Common prayer, fasting and pilgrimage to Mecca create a feeling of belonging which cannot be found in any of the other great religions. But this is also a solidarity of the weaker and the weak, since very few Islamic states have any economic power – from the production of oil. The West has little understanding of the problems of the Islamic world, which occasionally lead to really or apparently irrational political statements.

5

Art and Science in Islam

Religion has had a strong influence on the development of the arts among the Islamic peoples. Certain forms like painting and sculpture, literature and music, have tended to be neglected, whereas architecture reached great heights with the building of mosques, mausoleums and palaces. Of the sciences, medicine, astronomy and mathematics especially flourished in the Islamic kingdoms.

The commandment against making any images was interpreted very strictly in Islam. The period of the Umayyads and isolated periods in Persian and Indian history were exceptions here. However, the prohibition against images encouraged another art-form, calligraphy. From the seventh century, when the revelations to Muhammad, noted down in no particular order, were gathered together to become the Qur'an, skilled calligraphers vied in the aesthetic presentation of the sacred texts. As a script they used the old Semitic consonantal script of the Nabataeans, an Arabic-speaking people strongly influenced by late Roman culture, whose best-known creation is the rock city of Petra in present-day Jordan. This script not only served to communicate the content, but was also decoration. Two forms developed at a very early stage: Kufic script, which was angular and monumental, and Naskh script, round and flowing. The modern Arabic script developed from them. Surahs from the Qur'an were not only written on parchment but also chiselled on stone, cast in metal and baked on ceramic tiles. They are the decorative elements of mosques, mausoleums and madrasas (Qur'an schools), which contain no pictures. To the present day calligraphy is one of the most highly respected arts in the Islamic world.

The most striking achievements of Islamic art are works of architecture. The oldest Islamic buildings are mosques. They follow a basic pattern: a rectangular plan, great areas for prayer, which are often open-air courtyards, cupolas and minarets from which the faithful are called to prayer. In addition to the Great Mosque in Mecca, famous mosques include the al-Azhar mosque in Cairo and the mosques of Cordoba and Kairouan. Existing places of worship belonging to other religions often served as models or were taken over and transformed (the Umayyad mosque in Damascus, al-Aksa in Jerusalem, Hagia Sophia in Istanbul and Mogul mosques in India). In Jerusalem, Byzantine master-builders created the most beautiful monument of Islamic architecture, the Dome of the Rock. It is not a mosque, but was erected as a sanctuary over the rock on the Temple Mount which had been the base of the sacrificial altars of Abraham and David, and from which Muhammad had been taken up into heaven.

The Alhambra palace in Granada, Spain, gives an impression of the high level of secular building from the hey-day of Islamic civilization.

The hostility of orthodox Islam to music has crippled this great area of artistic expression. In literature the elevation of the Qur'an to being the greatest masterpiece in the Arabic language has clearly had an inhibiting effect on poets. Great literary works were written, not in Arabia, but in Persia and India. It is here that the famous 'Thousand and One Nights' originated. The decline of the Islamic world brought an increase in the illiteracy rate at a time when it was decreasing in Europe as a result of the invention of the printed book and the development of the school system. For a long time orthodox Islamic lawyers even forbade the building of printing works as 'un-Islamic'. So a culture of the spoken word, an art of popular narration, developed in the Islamic world – a paradox in a religion in which the written word, the 'book', enjoys an almost mystical reverence.

In the scientific sphere, religious precepts of Islam, like the lunar calendar, the fixed times of prayer, the fast of Ramadan and the direction of prayer, which had to be observed strictly, encouraged astronomy and geometry. Numbers and mathematics were taken over from Egypt. Fractions, roots and algebra are Arabic developments. Medical writings by Greeks (Hippocrates and Galen), philosophical works (Plato, Aristotle) and scientific works (Archimedes, Hero of Alexandria) were translated into Arabic and studied. Many writings from antiquity were only preserved in this way.

In the most flourishing periods of Islamic history, the science and arts were often at a higher level than in contemporary Europe. The political collapse of the Islamic world also led to a visible decline in these spheres of civilization. Artistic expressions which are more closely connected with the belief of Muslims are among the most important culture achievements of humankind.

For Further Reading

Gerhard Endress, *An Introduction to Islam*, Edinburgh University Press 1988

John L. Esposito, *Islam. The Straight Path*, Oxford University Press ²1991

H. A. R. Gibb, *Islam: A Historical Survey*, Oxford University Press ²1980

Shaykh Fahdlalla Haeri, *The Elements of Islam*, Element Books 1993

L. P. Harvey, *Islamic Spain 1250 to 1500*, Chicago University Press 1991

Albert Hourani, *A History of the Arab Peoples*, Faber 1992

Jacques Jomier, *How to Understand Islam*, SCM Press and Crossroad Publishing Company 1989

W. M. Watt, *Muhammad: Prophet and Statesman*, Oxford University Press ²1977

Two translations of the Qur'an are:

The Koran, translated by N. J. Dawood, Penguin Books 1959, and

The Message of the Qur'an, translated and explained by Muhammad Asad, Dar al Andalus, Gibraltar 1984, which is perhaps the best English translation for serious study.

The Hadith are available in M. Nawawi, *The Forty Hadith*, Holy Koran Publishing House 1977

Chronological table

CE		
570	Birth of Muhammad	Langobard empire in Italy, Avar empire on the Danube
662	Hijra (departure) of Muhammad to Medina	War between Byzantium and Persia; Carolingians in France prepare to establish a position of power
632	Muhammad dies in Medina	Slav empire of Samos in Eastern Central Europe
634–644	Muslims conquer Egypt, Palestine, Syria, Mesopotamia and Persia	Irish monks Christianize England; last Merovingian king in the Frankish empire (Dagobert)
656–661	Beginning of the 'Shi'a'	Croats and Serbs settle in the western Balkans
661–750	Umayyad dynasty	732: Charles Martel victorious over the Arabs
755	Spanish Umayyad dynasty (Emirate of Cordoba, to 1031)	Pepin crowned king, beginning of the Papal States

1099	Crusaders capture Jerusalem	Cistercian order founded
1187	Sultan Saladin destroys the Crusader kingdom	Frederick Barbarossa (1152–1190)
1359	Sultan Murad I, beginning of the conquest of the Balkans by the Turks	Charles IV regulates the election of the German king by the 'golden bull'; in 1348 founds the University of Prague
1389	Battle on the Amsel field, Turks conquer the kingdom of Serbia	Hapsburgs recognize the Swiss Confederacy
1453	Turks capture Constantinople	Gutenberg prints the Bible Hundred Years' War between England and France
1529	Turks besiege Vienna	1530 Charles V crowned emperor by the Pope
1571	Battle of Lepanto, Turkish fleet destroyed	Huguenot massacre in France; rebellion in the Low Countries
1683	Turks besiege Vienna	Peter I Czar in Russia
1718	Austria recaptures Belgrade and other Balkan territories from the Turks	Foundation of New Orleans by the French
1878	Austria occupies Bosnia and Herzegovina	Roumania, Serbia, Bulgaria and Montenegro independent

1924	Caliphate in Turkey abolished; Ibn Saud conquers Mexico	Death of Lenin
1948	Foundation of Israel, first Arab-Israeli war	Berlin blockade
1952	Libya independent; Hussein king of Jordan	First American hydrogen bomb; Eisenhower President
1967	Six Day War	Military coup in Greece
1969	First Islamic summit conference	First landing on the moon
1973	Yom Kippur War	Military coup in Chile
1978	Peace between Israel and Egypt	Vietnam invades Cambodia
1979	Revolution in Iran	Soviet invasion of Afghanistan
1980	Beginning of Iraq-Iran war	Reagan elected US President, Solidarity founded
1981	President Sadat of Egypt murdered	Martial law in Poland
1989	Death of Khomeini	Revolution in Eastern Europe